T0209310

ECHOES

FROM
GOLGOTHA

*Seeking the Mind of Christ
in the Place of the Skull*

OSCAR YTURRIAGA

WESTBOW
PRESS®
A DIVISION OF THOMAS NELSON
& ZONDERVAN

WestBow Press books may be ordered through booksellers or by contacting:

WestBow Press
A Division of Thomas Nelson & Zondervan
1663 Liberty Drive
Bloomington, IN 47403
www.westbowpress.com
844-714-3454

Cover designed by André Goboi

ISBN: 979-8-3850-0467-6 (sc)
ISBN: 979-8-3850-0468-3 (hc)
ISBN: 979-8-3850-0466-9 (e)

Library of Congress Control Number: 2023914762

Print information available on the last page.

WestBow Press rev. date: 11/06/2023

To Megan, my beloved wife and best friend.
This book would not have been possible without
your unwavering belief and continual support.

C O N T E N T S

FOREWORD

I often encourage those who love scripture to, at least once a year, complete this simple exercise. Write out all the statements of Jesus while He was both perched and pierced on Golgotha. Once down on paper, take a minute to slowly repeat each statement aloud. You'll find they barely fill one minute of spoken conversation. Just seven one-liners! Now imagine the dead space during those six hours as Jesus hung from the cross. Sure, other dialogue happened. There were two thieves who played some kind of theological word tennis over and around the Savior. Volleying their innuendos about the merits of a Savior who couldn't seem to save Himself. One of those thieves decided to double down on his pathetic attempts to do what even Satan himself couldn't do, distract Jesus from His mission. Hey, Jesus, "Save Yourself!" (Luke 23:39 NIV). The other thief broke from the pack; he began to melt. He did the best thing any human being can do. He stopped looking at other thieves and put his eyes (and requests) on Jesus. "Remember me" (Luke 23:42 NIV). Turns out those might be the two greatest words in human history.

There is so much Jesus could have said leading up to Golgotha. He could have ended the opening argument of His extradition with an ear-splitting sermon or offered up a plateful of prophetic thunder as a parting shot for Pilate. He could have unloaded an earful at the elders, or at least told Barabbas he was the luckiest parolee on earth. He could have requested a two-hour pass to go preach Judas Iscariot's funeral. The activists who hung a joker's sign over His scalp could have had the Mark of Beast tattooed on theirs. The one who rolled sixes for his clothes, along with the crown craftsman, the sword salesman, and the vinegar vendor, every last one of them could have gotten an illustrated ten-point sermon on hell. Jesus could have undressed with righteous rhetoric the Roman cohorts who stripped Him of his clothes, or showered condemnation on those who showered Him with their spit. He could have bellowed out a few shots from the book of Jeremiah or ordered up a few hungry bears like Elijah.

With his name and legacy being blasphemed on Golgotha, you wonder if Jesus ever squinted through the crimson veil to ask Himself if this was all worth it, wondering if His flock of fierce and loyal lambs were coming. Strewn across Galilee like wind-blown confetti were swarms of nameless and faceless individuals who had rehabilitated by His compassionate touch. Where were the righteous rioters? The former deaf should have heard the hammer pounding the nails. The former blind should have seen the shimmering sword-bearing centurions ... but there were no sounds, no movements, no mutiny, no insurgence. All that was left was a slow, quiet standoff between religion and sunrise.

Yet the Bible says, "When He was reviled, He did not revile in return; when He suffered, He did not threaten" (1 Peter 2:23 ESV). In the natural, Jesus's actions made no sense. When taunted, He remained tight-lipped. When abused and pierced, His words of forgiveness flowed as quickly as His blood. He didn't require His wounds to dry, scab, and scar before He forgave. There is no record that Jesus calculated His personal pain before discharging his pardon. Each bruise and blow were met with silence and mercy. In taciturnity, Jesus was doing more than dying. He was communicating in red ink the unending secrets of the kingdom. He was openly showing His bride how to embrace the cross that awaited her—because no true disciple can escape the cross.

Satan didn't see this coming. The longer Jesus hung in there, the more foolish Satan began to look—this leisurely six-hour crucifixion had completely backfired. It's tough to take the high road when people are spitting on you. But there was victory in the body language of Jesus. For all the strains and traumata this life brings, I will never pay a toll like Jesus. His death on Golgotha, along with His resurrection, provide me with the grace and perplexity to keep me both whole and curious.

For it was I, not Jesus, who should have died for violating my Creator's commands. And it was I who deserved the burden of transporting heavy timbers barefoot over jagged hillsides for my iniquity. It was I who merited loud public laughter and the agony of thorns stabbing my forehead—and it was I who should have felt my ribs being impaled as pagan spit dripped from my face. Yes, it was I who should have hung incapacitated for six millennia, not simply six hours. Yet it was Jesus, not I, who sadistically became my silent payment on that signature hill known only for its resemblance to the human skull.

So, as you read this wonderful work on Golgotha, keep Good Friday and Easter in their right order. Suffering is like John the Baptist; it prepares the way. Then remember again and again—and again, the great eternal paraphrase. The sermon involving of seven one-liners. The one that lasted six hours. The one that's easy to memorize but difficult to imitate.

Golgotha matters.

Scott Hagan, PhD
President, North Central University

So they took Jesus, and He went out, bearing His own cross, to the place called the Place of the Skull, which is called in Hebrew, Golgotha. There they crucified Him, and with Him two others, one on either side, and Jesus between them.
—John 19:17–18 (AMP)

THE STAGE

It was an ordinary Tuesday in November as I was making the seventy-five-mile drive from my church to meet with a small group of other pastors from across the state of Iowa for a much-needed time of encouragement and peer-to-peer ministry. I remember it well. My soul was weary after enduring a long and arduous stretch of leading the church through a season marked by a devastating global pandemic, polarizing political crises and incendiary racial tensions that had created a collective pressure cooker for leaders in every sphere of life.

Churches had been especially hard hit, many struggling just to keep their doors open. Large numbers of pastors had left the ministry, with burnout plaguing pulpits at an alarming rate. Friends and colleagues were disconcerted and deconstructing their faith, some walking away from Christ entirely and abandoning all they had once held sacred. Many churchgoers who withdrew from church life during this season still hadn't returned, and it was unclear if they ever would. These were times of life and ministry unlike anything we'd seen before. While most were eager to return to a sense of normalcy, there was a growing belief that this was simply going to be the new normal.

I was about half an hour from my destination when I experienced what I can only describe as an incredibly unique encounter with the Lord. I had been listening to the Gospel of Mark in my truck when suddenly it was as if the Holy Spirit had begun a high-speed download of fresh revelation into my heart. As soon as I could, I pulled off the road into the nearest gas station to begin writing down everything I heard God say. And within just a few minutes, I had the fully formed structure for the book you're now reading, complete with title, chapter headings, and the leadership concepts I'm about to share.

This was all so unexpected for me, as I had never written a book before, nor did I have any aspirations to do so. I'd only been a lead pastor for a little over five years at the time, and by no means have I ever considered myself to be a leadership guru. But there I was, jotting down notes, trying to keep up with the rapid-fire pace at which God was communicating. When I had finished transcribing, I so badly wanted to continue writing, but I needed to finish driving to a meeting that would prove to be the start of some of the most life-giving relationships I'd been privileged to enjoy, with comrades who truly understood the battle, and now I was going to be late.

Several months passed before I finally resumed writing, but all the while, I had this persistent compulsion in my spirit to write that I just couldn't ignore. And what so burdened my heart throughout that season was this question: "How can we lead with clarity and conviction in a time marked by uncertainty and cynicism toward the church?" In recent years, the church has been rocked by scandal after scandal, and the moral failures of many well-known ministers have been chronicled publicly for all the world to see. Exposés were written, documentaries have been produced, and ministries once thought to be unshakeable have been shaken to their core. I figured, surely the Lord has a way forward through this mess. After all, aren't God's people called to bring the solutions of heaven to the problems plaguing the earth?

As I pondered the answers to our present-day dilemmas, I was reminded of the early disciples who were often perplexed by much of Jesus's leadership on earth. Many would end up abandoning Him because they found His ways so incompatible with their wants. In the wake of His death, rather than boldly taking the Gospel into all the world, the eleven remaining disciples hid together behind a locked door, confused and afraid. Along the Emmaus Road, the resurrected Christ appeared and gave the disciples fresh insights that helped them understand the way of the cross. From that moment forward, the posture of their lives dramatically shifted from one of self-preservation to one marked by incredible sacrifice, altering the course of human history forever.

Could it be that when we lead from our own understanding, we'll inevitably run from the very things Jesus is calling us to embrace? While many believe the way forward is to look to new ideas and adapt our leadership to the challenges of our day, the reality is that the finished work of the cross is still complete, God's grace is still sufficient, and His power is still made perfect in our weakness. If our lives are going to impact eternity, I would submit to you that we must make it our highest goal to return to Golgotha, where death sets the stage for God's plan to once again burst forth with vibrant life and beauty in a dark and desperate world. I believe God is calling us back to the timeless truth of scripture to once again seek the mind of Christ in the place of the skull.

For three years, beginning in 2013, my family and I had the privilege of enjoying life and ministry on the beautiful Hawaiian island of Kauai. From its emerald mountain peaks to its pristine white sand beaches, I'm firmly convinced that God did some of His best work when He created this geological masterpiece! During our time on Kauai, we visited the beach often. From Hanalei Bay on the north shore to Polihale State Park on the west end, we enjoyed incredible views of ocean life with frequent appearances of monk seals and Hawaiian sea turtles. Tours of the remote Napali Coast had dolphins leaping and spinning behind the boat as we rode past stunning cathedral cliffs and majestic waterfalls. Atop Waimea Canyon, at more than 3,000 feet above sea level, we took in panoramic vistas of the island's dramatic interior and caught a bird's-eye view of the deep blue sea that extended all the way out beyond the horizon. Complete with remarkable rainbows, lava rocks, and puka shells, we took it all in and absolutely loved every minute!

After living on Kauai for a little more than a year, we were visited by some close friends from the mainland. While hosting them for several days, we wanted to share with them all of the beauty Kauai had to offer, so they too could experience the sense of awe and wonder produced by this special place. We planned as many excursions as we could, introducing them to much of the island as we'd come to know it. We drove them from one shore to the other, introducing them to out-of-the-way attractions often hidden from the average visitor to the island. For the most part, the tourist experience had gone according to what we had planned and predicted. But it was during one particular outing to Poipu Beach near our home when everything unexpectedly shifted.

My family and I had visited Poipu Beach so many times that we'd honestly lost count. It was the perfect little family spot where the waves were relatively small, the swimming was safe, and the typical tourist shops were plentiful. This was the perfect place to take visitors for spectacular sunsets and fabulous photo opportunities. While we were there, however, my friend Andrew had the idea to rent snorkel gear and venture a bit deeper into the water. Strangely, I'd never done this before on Kauai, but I was definitely up for doing something different. So, with all of the necessary equipment now in hand, we left the familiarity of the shallow waters to head out into the deep.

While I wasn't sure what to expect, the moment I submerged myself into the deeper waters, I peered out through my goggles to witness schools of fish swimming by that were more colorful and exotic than I could've imagined possible. Vibrant coral reefs teaming with life swayed back and forth with the rhythms of the ocean as rays of sunlight refracted through the waves above. Sea turtles that had appeared lazy and lethargic on the surface were now showing themselves to be nimble navigators of this aquatic atmosphere. Suddenly, it dawned on me that my experience of the island to this point had barely scratched the surface of all there was to see. How limited my view had been! How shallow my understanding of things! As I swam through this otherworldly habitat, I'll never forget what happened next. It was like a thousand tiny needles were piercing my skin all at once, and I quickly flashed back to the warning signs I'd seen posted about the Portuguese man-of-war jellyfish. Panicked and in pain, I exited the water so quickly I lost one of my flippers as I screamed in Andrew's direction, hoping to warn him in time.

Andrew made it out of the water without incident, and to this day we share a good laugh anytime we reminisce about what happened. But this experience got me thinking about just how often we approach the familiar with a sense of hyper-confidence and predictability, not realizing how limited our understanding truly is. The Gospel is no exception—having become so familiar to us that we may assume to have seen it all, but in reality, there are greater depths we've never ventured into. My experience with the Lord that day in the truck gave me a glimpse into a world I'd never fully explored, where what I thought I knew would no longer be sufficient in preparing me for the revelation I would receive. God was inviting me to go deeper.

In the final chapter of Luke's Gospel, there appears an incredible story about two men, distraught over the death of Jesus, who found themselves in deep conversation with the Messiah, only they didn't realize it was Him. There, as they walked the road to Emmaus, these two men learned about God's plan of salvation directly from the Savior Himself. Little did they know at the time, but Jesus was inviting them to go deeper with Him. After they'd arrived at their destination and were preparing to enjoy a meal, Jesus suddenly allowed the men's eyes to be opened before He vanished from their sight. After He'd gone, they asked themselves, "Didn't our hearts burn within us as He talked with us on the road and explained the Scriptures to us?" (Luke 24:32 NLT). It would seem that it took a little time for their heads to catch up with their hearts, but once they finally did, they gained a newfound perspective on the events of Golgotha.

We see a similar encounter later that day, as the two men met together with the other disciples in Jerusalem and shared with them what had happened. While they were speaking, Jesus suddenly appeared once again, and He proceeded to engage their doubt and disbelief with revelation of the things written about Him in the Law of Moses, the prophetic writings of the Old Testament, and the Psalms. Then, in verse 45, we're told that Jesus "opened their minds to understand the Scriptures" (Luke 24:45 NLT). These men had known these writings and were familiar with what they said about the promised Messiah. They were present for the life and ministry of Christ here on the earth, and they were well acquainted with the crucifixion. Yet there were still revelations they had missed—ways in which their minds hadn't yet been opened to fully understand.

While the cross is certainly empty today, its message continues to speak loudly to whoever will listen to what it has to say. The Lord is looking for those with their eyes open to what He's doing and their ears attentive to what He's saying in this hour. As you're reading this now, wherever you may be, do you sense deep down inside that there has to be more richness to the Christian life than what you've seen? Do you feel that there needs to be greater Gospel clarity in a world that's more confused than ever? Do you see a great need for the church to rise up with renewed strength and beauty to shine as the radiant bride God intended in the midst of this dark world? I believe Jesus is once again inviting us to go deeper—that He's joining us on our journey to talk with us and explain the scriptures to us, that our hearts might once again burn with revival fire.

It's my hope that you'll approach the pages of this book like a long walk with Jesus—that you'll listen for His voice and respond to what He stirs in your spirit. It's my prayer that you'll move out of mediocrity and away from apathy as you intentionally expose yourself to the righteous discomfort of the cross. And it's my deep desire that an overwhelming lovesickness for the Bridegroom would grip your life, causing you to give yourself away day by day in eager anticipation of His soon return. At the end of each chapter, a set of reflection questions is included as a resource for personal enrichment or group discussion. These questions are designed with one goal in mind: to help you follow decisively in the footsteps of Christ—that you would live full but die empty.

I realize this journey isn't one that'll appeal to the masses, and that's okay. I believe God's simply looking for a remnant few who'll be set apart for Himself, and I wonder if that might be you. If so, I'd like to pray for you. Heavenly Father, thank You for the hunger You're stirring in Your people for more. Lord, I ask that You'd use these feeble words of mine to somehow ignite holy fire. I ask that You'd meet your sons and daughters right where they are and take them where You're leading. I ask for a sovereign move of Your Spirit to revive the way, reveal the truth, and redeem each life for Your glory. In Christ's strong and righteous name, I pray. Amen.

CHAPTER 1

THE MANTLE

Jesus had just concluded the last supper with His disciples when He said these words to them, "The time has come for this prophecy about me to be fulfilled: 'He was counted among the rebels.' Yes, everything written about me by the prophets will come true" (Luke 22:37 NLT). Here, Jesus was quoting Isaiah 53:12 (NLT), which goes on to say, "He bore the sins of many and interceded for rebels." This prophetic image was about to become reality at the place of the skull. Later, at His arrest, Jesus would say to those who'd come for Him, "This is your moment, the time when the power of darkness reigns" (Luke 22:53 NLT). Jesus knew what the prophets of old had written. He understood full well what ugliness was being exposed. Yet He also had perfect clarity about the beauty that would emerge from it, which is why He could confidently declare, "You will see the Son of Man seated in the place of power at God's right hand and coming on the clouds of heaven" (Mark 14:62 NLT). Jesus was the light of heaven bursting forth into a dark world to reveal God's plan. *And what the enemy thought could extinguish the light would only intensify its radiance.*

At the outset of the crucifixion story, we're introduced to a passerby named Simon from Cyrene, who carried Jesus's cross. Three of the four Gospel writers include this detail in their accounts, briefly mentioning Simon. John's account differs from the rest, however, as he omits any mention of Simon, instead stating that Jesus carried His cross all by Himself. At first glance, some might argue that this presents a contradiction in the Gospel narrative. However, what most scholars agree upon is that John is merely writing about the beginning of Christ's journey as He carries His cross toward Golgotha, whereas the others included much more detail of what transpired during the journey. What emerges as these accounts are pieced together is the picture of Jesus carrying His cross until He could do so no longer, being assisted by this unlikely and unexpected character who seems to vanish from the story just as quickly as he had appeared.

So what do we know about Simon from Cyrene, and what are we to learn from his inclusion in the crucifixion scene? Presumably, Simon was seized by the Roman soldiers to carry the cross because Jesus's human body had already been stretched beyond its physical limits due to the intense flogging He'd endured beforehand. Crucifixion was intended to be a public spectacle that brought shame and disgrace to those who had broken the law, which is why Jesus and the two others were paraded through the streets. Scripture tells us that Simon walked behind Jesus as they were led up the hill to Golgotha, which certainly would've given him a very unique perspective.

As he quite literally walked in the footsteps of Jesus, Simon would have witnessed the righteous women weeping, the vicious people taunting, and following so closely behind Jesus, Simon probably would have felt as though all of this attention was being paid to him as well, giving him a secondhand taste of the burdens Jesus carried. It's widely believed that Simon, likely a Jew from the northern African region now known as Libya, was en route to Jerusalem for Passover. The father of two sons, Simon was thrust into this unwanted position that would now render him unclean and unable to engage in any of the festivities or ceremonies of Passover. He didn't choose this position; rather, it was chosen for him, and now there was nothing he could do about it. Tradition tells us that Simon would go on to become a missionary, spreading the Gospel throughout Egypt, ultimately giving his life for the cause of Christ in martyrdom.

The symbol of death that Simon carried on this day to Golgotha would be the very mantle that's placed upon anyone who would follow Jesus thereafter—a mantle that interrupts our path, requiring us to deny ourselves, and giving us a taste of the burdens of our Savior. The mantle of leadership in the kingdom of God doesn't discriminate, and it doesn't select us based on our abilities, ambitions, or list of accomplishments. Rather, the mantle God places on His servants still finds us in some of the most unexpected places. It takes us along the path of Christ, complete with a purpose that is still as powerful as it is painful. These inseparable realities of what it means to bear our own cross are an evidence that we're no longer following our own desires but that we've submitted our lives to a master greater than ourselves who can still turn any grave into a garden.

If one were only to read John's account of Christ's crucifixion, they'd be completely unfamiliar with this poignant moment where Simon carries Jesus's cross. They'd be wholly unaware of the physical, emotional, and mental toll this surely had taken on Simon. And their timeline of the Gospel narrative would essentially skip from Jesus being sentenced to Him hanging on the cross. Much would be missed without the other Gospel writers' contributions. And I've found this is often how leadership is handled within Christian circles. Like John, we tend to skip over the painful and less than perfect moments in our journey. We omit the aspects of our story that took a physical, emotional, and mental toll as we journeyed along our path, often mantled with a weight we weren't prepared to carry as we followed Jesus to the place He was leading.

Some have speculated that John deliberately left Simon out of his writing because of concern that doubters would claim he'd been crucified in Christ's place by mistake, which then would have nullified reports of Jesus's resurrection. No one can know for sure whether or not that was the reason for John's omission, but what I do know is that we often sanitize our own stories for fear that in sharing our pain we may inadvertently cast dispersions on the church, giving doubters reason to reject the Good News. And as well intentioned as we may be in doing so, I fear all that we've accomplished is to create false expectations of ease for those who would attempt the journey after us. Think about it; without Simon, would we have a clear picture of what it really means to carry our cross? Without the details of your journey, can those watching your life and ministry have a proper understanding of the cost associated with carrying that mantle of leadership?

The front-row view Simon found himself with in the Gospel narrative really resonates with me as I reflect on my own journey in following Christ and stepping into leadership. My wife and I began our ministry in 2006 with immense enthusiasm and high expectations. Our love for the church and our trust of its leaders and methods couldn't have been greater. What we'd seen from a distance left us feeling nothing but reverence and respect. However, it wasn't long after we stepped into our ministry role within the local church that our eyes were opened to a much different reality up close, which caused us to feel as though we'd been punched in the gut and left gasping for air.

At the time, we had two children, ages five and seven, when we moved several states away from family and friends to take our first position in youth ministry. We began with about twenty students in a church that ran a hundred people or so on a Sunday morning. We weren't sure what to expect as we began; we just knew God had called us there. But within less than a year, the group had exploded to more than a hundred and twenty students, and the church was abuzz with excitement. People were taking notice, and many of our colleagues in the state told us what an incredible situation we were in. But behind the scenes, we knew something just wasn't right. And although we probably didn't want to accept it at the time, the church was in a very unhealthy place.

A little more than a year into our time at the church, we were invited by the lead pastor to attend the upcoming monthly board meeting. While staff members and ministry leaders weren't typically included in these meetings, we obliged our pastor's request and showed up at the scheduled time. As we sat in that room, unsure why we were even there, we could've never imagined what was about to take place. The pastor had been meeting with one of the board members privately for accountability, which we were aware of. What we didn't know is what that board member was about to blurt out in the meeting, which would instantly change everything for us and our ministry there.

The meeting was going along as we imagined most every meeting did, talking about things like budgets for ministry departments, facility needs, and vision for the future of the church. Then suddenly and without warning, this particular board member, who'd been the pastor's accountability partner, leaned across the table, pointed his finger at the pastor, and accused him of having lustful feelings toward my wife. I could hardly believe what just happened! It was as if I was having an out-of-body experience! But what came next shocked me even more. The pastor didn't say a single word to defend himself against these absurd allegations. We were excused from the meeting shortly thereafter. Immediately, I knew our time there, short-lived as it may have been, was sadly over.

There were no apologies or explanations offered. There was no disciplinary action taken or public comment made. It was just as if nothing had ever happened. But we knew we couldn't continue with business as usual and simply sweep it all under the rug. Our leadership had behaved dishonorably and broken trust. For us to stay through the dysfunction would be to be complicit in the sin. It would be to indoctrinate our children into an irrevocably broken system where they could be the next casualty. Yet leaving that place was one of the most difficult decisions we ever had to make. Bound to maintain our integrity, we never maligned our leadership. But leaving quietly meant we, too, would break trust, sever relationship, and harm innocent students we'd worked so hard to build up. Sadly, we would later come to learn that the ministry ultimately dwindled back down to the twenty or so students it had when we'd first come.

It hardly seemed fair—the guilty remaining comfortable while the innocent suffered. Perhaps I was naïve. I fully expected difficulty in pastoral ministry. But I largely expected it to come from somewhere "out there" rather than somewhere "in here." I wish I could say this was the last time we encountered this sort of gut-wrenching disappointment in church leadership, that it was contained to this place and these people. But the reality is it was just the first in a series of many ugly incidents. Adultery, embezzlement, deceit, molestation, hatred, pride, abuses of power, revenge, and cover-ups were just some of the many horrendous things we'd end up witnessing and walking people through as we continued along our ministry path with various leaders in a variety of places.

While there's no justifying or defending any of the depraved things we've seen and walked through with people over the past twenty-plus years of ministry, I can't help but be reminded of the depths of depravity Jesus encountered along His ministry path. And my heart finds consolation in the story of Simon that points to a cross-shaped mantle that's placed upon anyone who would follow in the footsteps of the Pierced One. We all set out to serve God with our own plans and expectations of what it'll be like, but only when our destination is Golgotha will our lives be mantled with a purpose greater than our pain. Only when we accept the invitation to die with Jesus can resurrection life and power be produced through us. Only when we take personal ownership of the cross are we able to forgive the debts owed *to* us because we're reminded of the price that was paid *for* us. What we should all find extremely terrifying is the idea of ministry without the mantle. Because the truth is it's only through righteous discomfort that we're able to provoke the church toward revival and the lost toward repentance. Anything less will only continue to produce dead religion, full of forms without power and Christians without crosses.

As we each carry our own cross, the grace of God rests upon our lives to release honor, to stay humble, to align with truth, and to resist the enemy's schemes to hook us into the deadly trap of offense. We must remind ourselves that we don't do these things to achieve a certain outcome. We do them for the same reason Jesus did—because of the joy set before us, a joy that's not contingent upon fairness or favorable circumstances but one that strengthens and sustains through even the darkest valleys and the hardest days. In fact, joy is such a valuable commodity in the kingdom that the Father took joy and set it before the Son, for which Hebrews 12:2 (NLT) tells us He not only endured the cross, but joy enabled Him even to disregard its shame.

Mocked, tortured, stripped, beaten beyond recognition, and left for dead by the very ones He'd come to save, Jesus endured the most horrific thing to ever happen in human history and was subjected to unimaginable shame, yet He determined the joy set before Him made it all worth it. When the Bible says, "The joy of the Lord is your strength" (Nehemiah 8:10 NLT), the strength it speaks of isn't just the fruit of things going well for us. The joy of the Lord is, as Pastor Bill Johnson said, "the internal combustion of the presence and activity of God that causes everything else to bow" in our lives as inferior to the reality of His Spirit at work on the inside of us, granting us strength to confront, rather than conceal our pain—to find healing through the hurt.

This is the deep and persistent truth the apostle Paul spoke of when he wrote that we can rejoice in our sufferings (Romans 5:3 ESV) because the joy produced by the presence and activity of God allows us to access joy in any and every circumstance. This is the joy the psalmist David spoke of when he prayed to the Lord, "Restore to me the joy of Your salvation, and make me willing to obey You." We can obey God and do hard things because of the joy set before us. Life could strip us of everything we have, but we're able to walk away with a smile and go get it again. Why? Because of this glorious truth that, unlike the mantle that rests *on* us, the joy of the Lord actually abides *in* us, fueling our every mission and motivation, assured that we who share in Christ's suffering will also share in His glory. If you're lacking this kind of joy in your life today, like David, why not ask God to restore it in you? To want it is a great start, but the reality is you won't obtain what you merely desire; you take possession only of that which you actively seek after. This joy is your inheritance, so you have the right to claim what's yours.

The road to Golgotha is long, and the weight of the mantle you carry is great. Make no mistake, the Christian life isn't just difficult; it's *impossible* in your own strength. Whether in marriage, ministry, or just the monotonous tasks of day-to-day life, you need a supernatural supply of joy to keep your fire alive. This joy serves as an evidence that you weren't created for boredom, burnout, or bondage but for the incomparable pleasure that comes with knowing God. Jesus was clear that "in this world you will have trouble" (John 16:33 NIV), which is why on the way to Golgotha, it's vital that you keep your sights set on the spoils of victory. That which is costly for you to attain will become a treasure worth defending. And when the joy of the Lord becomes your source of strength, troubles won't stop you because there's no stopping a man or woman who's made it their goal in life to show that Christ is more precious than life itself.

The place of the skull was the goal of Jesus, and thus, it must be the goal of the Jesus follower. Like Simon, you are being thrust into the story—to embrace the mantle placed upon you and the fullness of joy set before you to fulfill the divine purpose deposited within you for God's glory. In Matthew 16:24 (NLT), Jesus tells us that if we want to be His disciple, we must give up our own way, take up our cross, and follow Him. In other words, if we're only willing to do the things that give us life, then we'll miss out on divinely disguised opportunities to lay our lives down. Just as the cross had to precede the resurrection, following Jesus demands our death before we can truly live.

In your life right now, you may find yourself wondering what beauty, joy, or celebration could be forged from the challenging situations you face. Maybe you've been sold out by someone you trusted, stood beside, and cheered on; betrayed by those you've shared a pew with and defended. The truth is it's often less painful to be kicked by a stranger than to be kissed on the cheek by a betrayer. Jesus knows this fact all too well, and Hebrews 4:15 (NLT) assures us that He's shared fully in all our experience of temptation. He's shared entirely. In all our experience. Every hurt, every ache. See, in the midst of your pain, the deepest truth is that Jesus is with you. His strength at your side to weather these storms. His whisper in your ear, speaking in the most silent of hours. And His presence comforting you in your deepest pain.

In this hard season, God is wanting to take your shaking and forge something within you that's unshakable. As you rely on Him and lean into surrender, you choose a process of trust that results in what we as lovers of God pursue: looking more like Jesus. There's purpose to be found in your pain. Don't let shame, pride, fear, regret, or apathy con you into silence. God's not done with you yet! A mighty move of His Spirit and truth is at hand, and you are a part of seeing it come to fruition. There's power contained in your story that the enemy doesn't want you to release. In the midst of some of your greatest trials and frustrations, God is issuing you a holy invitation to yet again take up your cross and follow Him. Don't grow weary of busting through dead places to bring life. Instead, respond in faith and allow the Lord to redeem your heartache and use it to produce someone else's hope in Jesus, to heal their hurts in the same way He's healed yours.

God certainly didn't author the pain and hardship you've suffered at the hands of those who've abused, exploited, and abandoned you. However, God is birthing something new in you through those difficult seasons. Don't give up on your healing journey! There's a resilience that came out of that one season you thought you wouldn't survive, but you did. There's godly character that came out of that season when you had integrity when no one else was watching. There's humility that came out of the season where nothing went the way you wanted, but you surrendered to God and trusted His wisdom and power over your own. Be encouraged that there's an assignment that awaits on the other side of freedom! Everything the enemy wanted to use to harm you, God wants to redeem for your good and for His glory. He'll take who you really are and your real story, even the messy parts where He needed to rescue you, and use it to show people how He can come into their real lives and rescue them too.

REFLECTIONS

1. As Simon took up the cross, he sacrificially shared the burdens of his Savior. Jesus tells us in Matthew 16:24 (NLT) that each of us must take up our cross if we want to be His disciple. What are some ways Christ calls us to sacrificially share His burdens as we follow in His footsteps?

2. The cross of Christ is a picture-perfect demonstration of God's ultimate purpose. In it, we see both power and pain working together to accomplish God's plan for our good and for His glory. As we embrace the mantle God has placed upon our lives, we can be certain there will be pain along our path. Although God doesn't author our painful moments, the fact is He won't let them go to waste. How has God used the painful experiences in your life to help accomplish His plan?

3. Some of the ugly realities of church life mentioned in this chapter have understandably been responsible for turning people away from community. If you've been actively involved in a local church body for any length of time, you've probably witnessed or experienced some of these types of things for yourself. And in all likelihood, you weren't at all prepared for the heartache. How do you think the church can do a better job of engaging in dialogue around some of these difficult subjects to prevent people from having a false expectation of ease? Do you find in yourself a tendency to sanitize your story, leaving out some of the ugly stuff? If so, why is that?

4. As we follow in our Savior's footsteps toward Golgotha, the weight of the mantle that's placed upon us can only be endured

when we fix our eyes on the joy that's been set before us. That joy is an inheritance freely given, but it's costly to maintain. Opportunities to be offended come daily, but the price tag attached is great. Satan knows if he can get you to buy what he's selling, it'll cost you your joy and strip you of strength. How do you actively protect your joy? With so many opportunities to be offended, how do you avoid becoming ensnared by this trap?

CHAPTER 2

THE DRY TREES

Scripture is filled with agricultural metaphors, which it employs to convey God's saving message to us in a way that we can understand. Jesus seemed especially fond of such imagery as He taught on the kingdom and the coming judgment. In Luke, chapter 23, we see more detail of His march to Calvary's hill as He interacts with a group of grief-stricken women who He refers to as "Daughters of Jerusalem" (Luke 23:28 TPT). As Jesus instructs these women not to weep for Him, He speaks prophetically to them about the days that are coming that will result in unspeakable devastation.

While there are certainly historical and eschatological applications of this text that are worthy of discussion as it pertains to Israel and the peoples of the world, what I'd like to key in on here is the metaphor Jesus uses in verse 31, where He says, "If this is what they do to the living Branch, what will they do with the dead ones?" (Luke 23:31 TPT). Or as several other translations refer to them, the dry [trees]. As the disciples reflected on this statement, it no doubt conjured memories of a similar metaphor Jesus used in John 15 when He referred to Himself as the vine and His followers the branches. Here, Jesus goes on to speak of two categories of branches: the fruitless and the fruitful. In verse 8, He says that only those who produce much fruit are His true disciples. The similarity is unmistakable—the dry trees and the dead branches; both disconnected from the source of life, both unfruitful. While someone may claim to follow Jesus and do His work, He's very clear that it is by our fruit that we will truly be known (Matthew 7:15–20 NLT).

Today, we have many different ways to evaluate the effectiveness of a church or ministry. Attendance of the Sunday-morning gathering, followers on social media, online viewership, giving, volunteerism, outreach programs, community reputation, the number of campuses, and the quality of the facilities. All of these are measures people use to quantify fruitfulness. The trouble is you can achieve all of those benchmarks and still be a dead tree. If you contract with the right consultants, follow the prescribed formulas, build around charismatic personalities, and have just the right look, you too can construct your own kingdom complete with recognizable branding, catchy songs, and viral content.

In Luke 19, we see the triumphant entry of Jesus into Jerusalem, which of course occurred just five days prior to His crucifixion. Crowds gathered, prophecies were fulfilled, and a chorus of praises were lifted in jubilant celebration. It was a revival atmosphere, yet we see Jesus wept over the people because they had missed the time of God's coming (Luke 19:41–44 NIV). The living Branch was among them, but all they could see were the dead ambitions of an earthly kingdom that would give them a sense of self-importance and influence. They saw the appeal of following Jesus to greater things but neglected to recognize that Jesus Himself was the greater thing. Greater than the most gifted orator. Greater than the best band. Greater than revival. Greater than religion. And greater than any earthly kingdom that can ever be set up.

See, we can look to a lot of things—things that aren't necessarily bad, but if we're not careful, we can allow those things to cause us to miss the most important thing and not even realize it. Luke tells us there was a large crowd of disciples joyfully praising God in loud voices for all the miracles they'd seen. But in just a few days' time, when Jesus was being crucified on Golgotha, we find only John the beloved and a handful of women mentioned who followed Him there. Why? Because the reality is that the cross has a way of thinning out a crowd, separating fans from followers. Sure, the crowds were loud when Jesus was teaching, feeding, and healing. But Jesus knows the difference between those who are loyal and those who are just loud.

Everybody can get excited about seeing miracles, having a nation that's ruled by King Jesus, having throngs of people shouting, "Hosanna," and waving palm branches. But Jesus's tears tell us a different story, don't they? As He weeps over Jerusalem, we're reminded that if we aren't careful, we too can run the same risk. Coming to church, singing praises to God, praying for God to save our nation, and even experiencing the miraculous in our midst. Yet Jesus may in fact weep over us too because we're looking to all those things instead of looking to Him. And in our rush to resurrection, like the many disciples who scattered, our faithfulness can be fickle when God's plan looks different from ours. We all want the empty tomb, but are we willing to walk the difficult path to Golgotha?

Not only was Jesus filled with sorrow as He wept over the people of Jerusalem and their rejection of His salvation, but Mark 11:15 (NLT) shows us that as He came into the temple courts, He was also filled with a righteous anger. He began flipping tables because of what He saw happening there—a broken and corrupt religious system that claimed to give people access to the source of life, but all they had to offer were dry trees. And not only was Jesus incensed by what *was* happening in the temple (the money changing and the selling of things like doves), He was also upset about what *wasn't* happening there. Specifically, Jesus cites two issues: (1) they hadn't devoted themselves to prayer; and (2) they hadn't opened it up for all people to have access to God. As we consider what made Jesus weep, we must also consider what made Him flip tables. And it wasn't what was going on out in the world; it was what was happening in His Father's house.

As I sat in my living room in the spring, preparing my sermon for Palm Sunday, I was studying this portion of Luke's Gospel when the glory of God invaded that place in a special way. I quickly found myself weeping, face down on the floor. And I heard the Lord say two things. The first thing I heard Him say was, "I am cleansing the temple courts once again. No longer will they be consumed with the busyness of religious activity and plagued by hypocrisy." And secondly, I heard God say, "The Dove is not for sale! My Spirit isn't attracted to man's empty extravagance and elaborate designs. My presence comes to those who pray." This rocked me to my core! It was in that moment I realized that until I become righteously angered by the things that anger God, I can never become a deliverer of anything.

I shared what God had put on my heart in the sermon that Palm Sunday, and there was a tangible presence of the Lord in that place. This message that had been birthed through tears was unlike any I'd preached in recent memory, and to be honest, I was beyond relieved when it was over! I thought, *Okay, Lord. I did it, so now I can be done. Now I can go back to how things were before—comfortable and controlled.* Well, that's not exactly how things played out because I'm telling you, as soon as I came home and sat down in the living room, God began speaking to me again, just like before. And He told me what He was about to say was a word for the church.

This is what I heard: "This will be a year that will one day be looked back on and remembered as the year that celebrity Christianity went to its grave. And in its place will be birthed a fresh new move of My Spirit marked by purity, humility, and fire. The new thing I am about to do will be unlike any move we've witnessed before, and it will restore the good reputation of Christ's bride. The term 'revival' carries with it a certain form from years gone by that won't adequately describe what's coming." As I pondered these things in my spirit, the word I kept hearing from the Lord was "groundswell." I looked up the *Merriam-Webster Dictionary* definition of that word, which reveals the double meaning of (1) a broad, deep undulation caused by a seismic disturbance; and (2) rapid, spontaneous growth.

The message continued: "The catalyst for what'll take place won't be charismatic personalities or gifted leaders. It won't be church-growth formulas or seeker-sensitive methods employed in the name of relevancy. This will be a sovereign move of My Spirit that no man will be able to take credit for and no man will be able to stop. A growing hunger within the body of Christ will lead to a global grassroots prayer movement that'll open the heavens in unprecedented ways. As a result, fresh oil will be poured out, and a new generation of leaders will arise out of places of obscurity with incomparable zeal and anointing. Their only goal being My glory."

He said, "No longer will the altar be traded for the stage. No longer will My church measure success in numerical terms. Deep spiritual wells are being dug in places where the land is dry and parched in order for new works to spring up where the doors of dead religion have been shut. Just as I cursed the fig tree, I am once again pronouncing death over whatever fails to produce life. I am once again cleansing the temple courts and calling My bride to consecrate herself in preparation for the coming of the Bridegroom." Wow, what a word from the Lord!

I'm reminded that when Jesus could've opted for the palms—the loud praises men offered as He rode into the city—instead He chose the thorns because He knew it was the only way for dry branches like you and me to be revived. Recently, we've seen too many instances of ministry leaders who've opted for the company and compliments of crowds. But in this season, Jesus is still calling His bride to follow Him past the praises of men, to the cleansing of the temple, and all the way to the thorns of Calvary's cross. Because resurrection power must always be preceded by a death. Don't miss the new thing the Lord's doing because of what it looks like now. Satan loves to take what's beautiful and ruin it. But God loves to take what's ruined and make it beautiful. Golgotha reminds us that our greatest days lie ahead. Now is the time to get ready for what's about to burst forth!

God's Word is resolute in the promise that the destiny of the church will outweigh her history. In the last days, scripture teaches that some will depart from the faith. However, in the last days, scripture also teaches that God will pour His Spirit out on all flesh. We mustn't stay focused on the departing of dry trees and dead branches. Instead, we need to remain focused on the pouring out that produces life and fruit in us. Yes, we need to deal with the areas crumbling around us, but we must rebuild according to the Word, not according to popular Christian culture. We have to get back our authenticity and power. We need to get our hands out of the cookie jar of religion and surrender to the leading of the Holy Spirit once again.

In 2 Timothy 3, we're given several warnings about what it'll be like in the last days. In verse 5, the apostle Paul warns that people "will act religious, but they will reject the power that could make them godly. Stay away from people like that!" (2 Timothy 3:5 NLT). In other words, the greatest enemy to the working of the Holy Spirit isn't the world. It isn't sinners. It's not politics, other faiths, or the media. The greatest enemy to the working of the Holy Spirit is the presence of the religious spirit at work in the church. Yet how many perceive the religious spirit as the threat that it is? How many pastors and leaders in the church placate and pacify those in their midst who operate under its influence, giving them platforms that poison through their influence? How much of the lifegiving Spirit is choked out by catering to their carnal demands?

By contrast, time and again in the Gospels, we read the accounts of demonic spirits manifesting when Jesus arrives on the scene. He had no interest in keeping the peace with those who operated under their influence. Instead, we see that He provoked them by standing firm in the truth, walking in both His full power and authority. If we aren't careful to follow Christ's example in this, we'll end up pacifying spirits we were meant to provoke, preventing the deliverance that could've resulted from their revealing. The fact is God delivers us from our enemies, not from our friends. As long church leaders befriend the religious spirit, our people won't be set free from this illegitimate authority ruling and reigning in God's house. We'll remain a collection of dry trees and dead branches with no life in us or fruit produced by us.

Authority and power are fundamental parts of the kingdom of God. In fact, the concepts are inferred in the very word *kingdom*. Our English term *kingdom* is actually a compound word derived from the phrase "king's dominion." It implies a king's royal right to rule. This concept of authority is foundational to an understanding of the kingdom of God. God's kingdom is the product of His authority. Backing God's authority is His power. These two are not synonymous. Whereas His power is His ability, His authority is His absolute right to exercise that power in the establishment of His will. God not only exercises His authority and power; He delegates both to His church. We have been given the keys to the kingdom, and we need to use them! The powers of intimidation must be broken, so spiritual fathers and mothers in the church can assume their roles and carry out their duties in protecting and nourishing the body, walking in the fullness of their God-given power and authority.

We must create unity around truth, or else we'll avoid difficult issues in the name of a oneness that's devoid of truth. Silence and passivity only leave room for deception to speak, convincing us that hiding from the division that exists is equivalent to solidarity. This is the difference between peacemakers and peacekeepers. You can't maintain what you haven't fought for to begin with. However, when you confront what has crippled you, you live with new boldness and confidence, inviting the same power and authority that marked Jesus's life and ministry to mark yours. When you stand on God's Word and are led by His Spirit, you will inevitably provoke the spirit of religion. Don't feel compelled to create an unholy unity with that demonic stronghold. The enemy will do his best to intimidate you, but if you stand firm in the authority of God's Word and remain resolute in the power of His Spirit, that enemy stronghold will break, and it'll be the moment you see the heavens open and your prayers go unhindered.

Here's what I envision for the church in the last days: Remarkable fruit will be produced, drawing a clear distinction between dead branches and those that remain connected to the vine. Those who embrace the new wineskin will be included in this great outpouring, as what's natural for man will give way to what's normal for God. Instead of using "I'm human" as an excuse to walk in the desires of the flesh, the body of Christ will begin using "I'm saved" as a reason to walk in the power of the Spirit. This will be a time when the church recognizes the realm of God's promises that lingers over the church and says, "Yes," to what could be. No longer will we try to do inside the four walls what we're called to do outside. No longer will we settle for being importers of culture, rather than exporters of the kingdom.

This will be the era when the remnant rises up with boldness and courage to complete the global assignment given to the church to prepare for the Bridegroom's return. An atmosphere of faith and fragrant worship will replace entertainment worship and powerless prayer. As the presence of the Lord takes priority over clocks and calendars, the ministry of the Holy Spirit will do in a moment what man couldn't accomplish in a lifetime. A new generation will get a taste of the upper-room encounter. Even as I write this now, revival is breaking out at Asbury University in Wilmore, Kentucky, and spreading to other colleges like Lee University in Cleveland, Tennessee, and Cedarville University near Dayton, Ohio. These young firebrands will be infused with freshly kindled spiritual hunger and vitality, never again settling for going through the motions of dry trees and dead branches. They'll speak with boldness and authority, commanding life to spring forth from places where death once reigned, redeeming the church and restoring the beauty of Christ's bride. A new Jesus revolution is upon us—it's spilling out into the streets, sweeping across the nation, and soon, I believe, this fire will spread to the ends of the earth.

REFLECTIONS

1. The indignation Jesus showed when God's people turned His Father's house into a den of robbers gives us a glimpse into the things that grieve His heart. The truth is that until we become righteously angered by the things that anger the Lord, we'll remain content with status quo, and consequently, we can't become a deliverer of anything. What things are upsetting to the Lord today that have become status quo in His house? How should we respond to His righteous anger?

2. The Lord wants to put to death anything that displeases Him in the church. He calls us to be holy just as God is holy (1 Peter 1:15 NLT). This should get us excited because we know God's getting ready to birth something new as He takes what's ruined and makes it beautiful. What gets you most excited about this season that the church is in? What do you see the Lord birthing?

3. If the greatest enemy to the working of the Holy Spirit is the presence of the religious spirit at work in the church, it's incumbent upon us in leadership not to pacify what God has positioned us to provoke. That being said, what do you see the Lord exposing in His church right now? What would it look like to surrender more control of our gatherings to the Holy Spirit?

4. When you think about spiritual fathers and mothers, who in your life comes to mind? Have you experienced the strength and diversity of a multigenerational spiritual family where people pour into one another? If this is a foreign concept to you or one you've never personally seen in action, doesn't that concern you? When God repeatedly speaks of the church in terms of

family, how can we justify the kind of corporate wineskin and consumerism so many have settled for?

5. If fruitfulness is the sign of a living branch that's connected to the vine, what does that say about you? What does it say about the health of the local body of Christ where you fellowship?

CHAPTER 3

THE REVOLUTIONARIES

Atop the hill of Golgotha, we can all picture the famous scene of three crosses in our minds, with Jesus at the center and two unnamed figures flanking Him on either side. The reason given for these men being executed can be found in the terms employed by the Gospel writers when referencing them, though verbiage may differ depending on the particular text and translation. Most have described these men as criminals. Many have called them robbers and thieves. However, some modern Bible translations of Matthew and Mark actually refer to them using the word *revolutionaries*, which according to Bauer's Greek-English Lexicon is a proper translation from the original Greek language. In fact, the same word used in the description of these men was also used to describe Barabbas, the infamous insurrectionist set free in exchange for Jesus to be crucified.

While we can't possibly know with certainty what their exact crimes were, the fact that these men were executed alongside Christ speaks to the gravity of their offenses and lends credibility to them being characterized as something other than common criminals. Though this makes little difference in the narrative from a historical standpoint, when we allow the change of language to shift our perception of their role, some powerful parallels emerge.

Accepting the premise that all three men crucified on this day were revolutionaries, we can logically conclude that although each man wanted to bring about significant change, they took radically different approaches to accomplish their goal, and only one of them actually achieved His in the end.

When we think of strong leaders, we tend to identify the loud, larger than life characters in charge of nations, armies, large corporations, or sports teams. However, these archetypal figures often known for their charisma, vision, and strategic leadership skills only describe a very small fraction of society. Most of us don't fit that definition and therefore have come to believe we're unqualified to be used significantly by God to lead others. But if Christ is our example, there's hope for all of us to find a place of significance in His kingdom because He defined leadership very differently. Jesus said to His disciples, "You know that the rulers in this world lord it over their people, and officials flaunt their authority over those under them. But among you it will be different. Whoever wants to be a leader among you must be your servant, and whoever wants to be first among you must become your slave. For even the Son of Man came not to be served but to serve others and to give His life as a ransom for many" (Matthew 20:25–28 NLT). This means that the type of servant leadership Jesus requires is attainable for us all.

Christ personified the ultimate servant leader, and His cross was the ultimate depiction of servant leadership, so shouldn't our greatest goal then be to learn as much as we can about leadership from Golgotha? Yet the majority of Christian books, programs, and podcasts available today on the subject of leadership seem to be taking their own revolutionary approach, having more in common with the crosses on either side of Jesus than the one He hung upon—borrowing concepts and structures of leadership from the world, rather than drawing from Christ's teaching and example. Golgotha illustrates for us the inescapable reality of leadership, that we'll always imitate the revolutionary we most admire. As followers of Jesus, it's imperative that we imitate not only His purpose but also His personality. This means redefining leadership so that our priorities no longer revolve around *what* we produce but rather around *who* we reproduce. Servant leadership never treats people as disposable, understanding that relational deposits may not always yield the results we expect, but they're never in vain. So to have the heart of Christ is to fight for the success of every relationship, though one may scorn you while the other celebrates you.

Something I wish someone had told me when I first stepped into ministry is that a Christian leader who speaks in a bullying, harsh, or demonizing way about other people (for any reason) frankly isn't acting like a Christian, and we shouldn't tolerate it. The truth is that the only people Jesus ever opposed were those who falsely claimed to represent His Father, or those seeking to profit off of His house—not politicians, not the sexually deviant, not everyday sinners. Those were the ones He actually befriended because loving them meant entering into their lives, listening to them, and actually caring for them. I'm not saying there isn't space to speak truth to those in the world, but we need to do so as Jesus did. He wasn't hateful or cruel. He didn't demonize those who disagreed with Him. So to do so is never Christlike—the world seems to know this intuitively, yet many in the church have been deceived by these other revolutionaries and their ungodly methods.

The flesh will always try to take control, and if we're honest with ourselves, we tend to prefer known variables and predictable outcomes because they produce a sense of security and comfort for us. But those things really don't require faith or courage. Real leadership is about stepping into the unknown, not the understood. The kingdom we belong to is an upside down one where we lose to gain and we die to live. If what we're doing makes perfect sense to everyone around us, the reality is we're probably doing something wrong. When will we stop settling for natural means that make sense to natural men? It's high time we accept the fact that still today only the King's approach can truly yield kingdom results, counterintuitive as it may often seem.

To think, the King of kings and Lord of lords stepped into time and space to take the form of a human. He could've been seated on a throne and reigned over all the nations of the earth, but instead He came as the Good Shepherd to care for a helpless flock and model for us what that's supposed to look like. In John chapter 10, Jesus is quoted as saying the following in differentiating between a hired hand and a shepherd: "A hired hand will run when he sees a wolf coming. He will abandon the sheep because they don't belong to him and he isn't their shepherd. And so the wolf attacks them and scatters the flock. The hired hand runs away because he's working only for the money and doesn't really care about the sheep" (John 10:12–13 NLT). Similarly, both Paul and Peter make appeals in their writings for elders and overseers to be true shepherds over their flock, both protecting and caring for the sheep (Acts 20:28, 1 Peter 5:1–2 NLT).

Perhaps one of the least understood aspects of church life is just how many wounded shepherds there are. Disappointment, discouragement, bitterness, and betrayal have sunken their teeth into more pastors and church leaders than probably any of us could count. A poll of pastors conducted by Barna Research Group in 2021 reveals that 38 percent have seriously considered quitting full-time ministry in the past year. That number was even higher (46 percent) among pastors under the age of forty-five. Among those who've considered quitting, 56 percent cited the immense stress of the job as a reason, 43 percent indicated feelings of loneliness and isolation, and 29 percent stated they weren't optimistic about the future of their church. Since the pandemic lockdown in 2020, over 1,700 pastors have been leaving the ministry every month. Make no mistake, our adversary is well aware of these statistics, and he's doing all he can to push pastors and church leaders over the edge—to divide, discourage, deceive, and ultimately destroy them.

For many who find themselves under attack and on the verge of burnout, the idea of becoming a hired hand can have its appeal. Those who opt for this route in response to their wounding will erect barriers for self-preservation. Creating distance between themselves and the flock, hired hands will often make themselves largely inaccessible, preferring to approach ministry like a CEO and treating the sheep as tools whose value is found in their ability to build the brand or reach numerical goals. And when things don't go well for the hired hand, they'll often lash out at the sheep they've failed to care for.

Truly, we are never more like the two revolutionaries crucified alongside Jesus than when we go the route of the hired hand—pursuing what's best for ourselves, professionalizing the ministry, and trusting no one. Settling for a transactional approach to church leadership, the hired hand refuses to engage on an emotional level. Unfamiliar with the sheep, they neither recognize the voice of the hired hand nor do they have the necessary protections of a shepherd who takes the time to get to know them on a relational level. Consumer Christianity flourishes in these environments, the enemy thrives through a political spirit, and isolation ultimately results in the demise of many who refuse to bring their private battles into the light of community, where healing and accountability can be provided.

The corporate, transactional approach to church leadership may produce results for a season, and many are likely to hold these leaders in high regard. However, seasons don't last forever, so it's only a matter of time before the walls built by the hired hand begin to crumble and the place of isolation that was meant for their protection becomes the means of their destruction. As wounding turns to insecurity, everything they see and hear becomes emotionally rearranged in their minds—everyone a potential enemy out to cause them further harm. Comparison wages war against their confidence, and soon the hired hand seeks to control the very people they were intended to empower, stifling growth and breeding animosity where they once enjoyed accolades.

Let me reiterate here that we'll always imitate the revolutionary we most admire. If we settle for imitating only Christ's purpose, we can easily be misled by a leader's charisma and passion, their gifts and performance. It's how instead of following the Shepherd on the middle cross, we end up being led by a hired hand who may look the part of Christ but lacks the heart of Christ. Only when we seek both the purpose of Jesus *and* His personality can we have our eyes opened to the red flags of wounded and insecure leaders who've traded their shepherd's crook in for a cattle prod. Those with the heart of the Good Shepherd embrace servant leadership, leading by example (1 Peter 5:3 NLT). Their desire is to feed, comfort, and protect the sheep as they lead them to greener pastures, to anoint their heads with oil and cause their cup to overflow in joy (Psalm 23:1–5 NLT). Their heart's cry is to love those Christ has given them just as He loves those the Father gave Him; therefore, serving in places of obscurity won't diminish their zeal or hinder their purpose. The banqueting table the Lord has set up before them is their source of satisfaction. To dine with Him is their great honor, and they never run out of room for others to pull up a chair.

The differences in methodology of the three revolutionaries that hung upon the crosses of Golgotha actually revealed vast disparities in their morality. Likewise, the difference between the shepherd and the hired hand goes well beyond the leadership methods they employ and reveals who's really fit for kingdom work. More than one's oratory skill, stage presence, and wit—of greater importance than the ability to motivate, inspire, and organize—is the heart to nurture the flock God has entrusted to the leader. Heaven has no shortage of supply when it comes to gifting and ability, but the heart of a servant is truly a rare and precious commodity that is sadly undervalued by many today.

When ministry is mentioned in the New Testament, the writers of scripture use the Greek word *diakonia*. This is the same root word from which we get the term *deacon*. Diakonia simply means "to be at one's service." Since Christ came not to *be served* but to *serve*, to minister in His name then is to do the very same thing—to be at one's service. Jesus was the ultimate picture of diakonia, so we should ask ourselves whose service He was at.

In Mark 12, a teacher of the law approached Jesus with the question "What is the greatest commandment?" Jesus's response was that it is to "love the Lord your God with all your heart, all your soul, all your mind, and all your strength" and to "love your neighbor as yourself" (Mark 12:30–31 NLT). This was Christ's definition of diakonia because in the kingdom, love is always accompanied by action. So love causes us first to serve God and, second, to serve people. What Jesus wanted us to understand here is that we must never be so focused on what God wants us to achieve for Him that we miss the revelation of who He wants us to become—humble servants, motivated by divine love. Anything other than this may be called "ministry" by man, but God looks upon it very differently.

To illustrate this point further, in John 13, Jesus does something that absolutely blows my mind—He washes the disciples' feet. Here the highest man in all the world takes the lowest position, bestowing undeserved honor and value on each one, not just the loving and loyal but even the doubter, the denier, and the betrayer. Afterward, He said these words, "Since I, your Lord and Teacher, have washed your feet, you ought to wash each other's feet. I have given you an example to follow. Do as I have done to you" (John 13:14–15 NLT). In many Western churches today, it seems we've managed to reduce the beautiful servanthood and sacrifice of Christ to a mere backdrop for our self-centered lives. But in verse 17, Jesus says, "Now that you know these things, God will bless you for doing them" (John 13:17 NLT). In other words, Jesus requires that we reject entitlement and instead take personal ownership for that which we corporately desire.

The fact is diakonia isn't just one of many different forms of ministry that are acceptable to God. No, it's the only one that counts—the only one that He'll bless. Anything else is a counterfeit in God's eyes. We must therefore reject the theology of cultural relevance. We'll never win the world by becoming like the world. The only way we can win the world is by becoming like Jesus, and that's a costly endeavor—requiring that we be set apart from the world, crucified to our own desires and treasuring the kingdom above all else. As J.C. Ryle said, "A religion that costs nothing is worth nothing. A cheap Christianity, without a cross, will prove in the end a useless Christianity, without a crown."

One of the great dangers facing us today is the entertainment model of church that creates and choreographs meetings where people are trained to become sedentary spectators of services, rather than dynamically moving in the gifts of the Holy Spirit. People remain deactivated, callings lie dormant, and hearts are tragically marked by cold indifference. Seekers come looking for otherworldly power but instead find only worldly productions. The bride of Christ anemically limps along, shaking her head at a world in darkness, oblivious to the radiance she's meant to display. Meanwhile, what's perhaps most tragic of all is that when there are butts in the seats and money in the coffers, many in the church call this success. I say these things not to belittle the bride of Christ but rather to lovingly call her up to the level of her potential. May we be reminded to live according to our true identity and refuse to settle for anything less. We are those who've been betrothed, dressed in eternal glory, and marked by an incurable lovesickness for our Bridegroom's return. If we define ourselves any other way, we forfeit parts of who we're meant to be and go on living a substandard existence that's powerless to revolutionize anything.

A church that continues to be dominated by self-help sermons, celebrity figureheads, and an entertainment culture offers no hope for a broken world desperate for the presence of God. The Western church model of leadership has often come to mean bigger, better, more, faster. Sadly, this doesn't seem to be the radical way of Jesus. In all of the metrics and measurements used to evaluate churches and ministries, we must be clear on this one thing—success isn't where we're going; it's where God is. Numbers, buildings, influence, reputation, and reach become entirely meaningless if it doesn't flow out of His presence. Like Moses, who saw the glory of the Lord and delivered God's people from the idol worship of a golden calf they'd named Yahweh (Exodus 32:5 YLT), when God becomes enough for us, our cry will be, "Lord, I would rather be in the wilderness with you than in the promise without You."

It's only God's presence that distinguishes us from any other social gathering or movement this world has ever known. We must return to presence-led life and leadership if we're going to be delivered from religious routine and passionless living. On the heels of the burnout and bailout that resulted from the era of Christian deconstruction, there's a remnant being raised up who are committed to crying out for a resurrection of The Way we read about in the pages of the New Testament. However, this isn't humanity's default response. Instead, in Numbers 32:1–7 (NLT), we see a story of God's people giving up on the Promised Land and settling for a land they had deemed suitable. I believe what the Lord is saying to the church today is that we mustn't settle for suitable when He offers us supernatural. We mustn't settle for results when He invites us into relationship. We mustn't settle for entertainment when He wants to give us encounter.

Has God gotten your attention yet, or are you still consumed by this machine we call church that just keeps cranking out replica after replica based on the latest church growth models? The bottom line is that we need much more Jesus and far less junk. While it might look tasty, the fact is that ordering off the fast-food dollar menu has never led a single soul to have improved health, and neither will feasting on imitation spirituality. In order for us to recapture the revolutionary nature of the New Testament church that we read about in the pages of scripture, it's imperative that we reject the ego-driven structures suffocating life out of the body. We must instead determine that our gatherings become centered on the presence of the Lord and be discontent with anything less than a demonstration of glory that'll conform us to the image of Christ. These five simple words should drive all that we do: "She had heard about Jesus" (Mark 5:27 NLT). This is what holds the power to transform lives—that they would hear, so when He shows up, they'll press through the crowd and grab hold of Him. This is everything!

To become like Jesus is to take on the heart of the Shepherd—one who's consumed with the revelation of how deep and how wide the love of God is. Shepherds are lovers of the New Covenant that invites the lost into the spirit of adoption. They're concerned with the least, the last, and the lowly. They're committed to loving them into the identity of family, to leading them into the purpose of kingdom, and to leveraging their healing to touch the hurting world that surrounds. As these shepherds approach people with a demonstration of genuine faith and love, knowing how to sacrifice and not just sermonize, they'll attract a generation to Christ. As they replicate themselves in others, they'll create a vibrant upper-room community that's unafraid of a little fire, hungry souls who knows how to fan a flame and stir up a gift. These disciples will become an army that knows how to fight hard and a family that knows how to love big—brothers and sisters who'll lower others through a roof to their healing, who'll worship people's chains to the floor when they're in bondage, who'll run to Jesus on behalf of the outcast and call that which is dead and dying to come forth out of an early grave.

Professionalized ministry, however, will never result in such an otherworldly outcome. As John Piper said, "The mentality of the professional is not the mentality of the prophet. It is not the mentality of the slave of Christ. Professionalism has nothing to do with the essence and heart of the Christian ministry. The more professional we long to be, the more spiritual death we will leave in our wake. For there is no professional childlikeness, there is no professional tenderheartedness, there is no professional panting after God." See, learning to *serve* is a prerequisite for being a shepherd. But take note, the prerequisite for being a servant is learning to *seek*. You're an image-bearer with work to do, not a work-doer with an image to maintain. Ministry was never meant to be a stress and a strain, yet we see so many church leaders plagued by anxiety, carrying an enormous weight. You'll never be able to minister from a place of emptiness. This is why Jesus says, "*Seek* first the Kingdom" (Matthew 6:33 NIV), not "*serve* first the Kingdom." If you serve first, you'll quickly burn out. Many a servant has lost their joy because they prioritized *doing* over *being*. Remember, Jesus extended the invitation of "Come to Me" (Matthew 11:28 NLT) before He issued the instruction of "Go for Me" (Matthew 28:19 NLT).

The formula of the kingdom is still the same today—mission must always be fueled by presence. If you get your priorities backward, you'll find yourself running dry, but when you do things God's way, your cup runs over, and you're able to minister out of the overflow of all that He's poured into your heart. One of my favorite passages in all of scripture is Psalms 25:14, and I love the way The Passion Translation reads. It says, "There's a private place reserved for the lovers of God, where they sit near Him and receive the revelation-secrets of His promises" (Psalms 25:14 TPT). Did you catch that? You don't need to wait in line. You don't have to pay an upgrade fee for a better view. You have reserved seating near God Himself. What a beautiful picture that conjures imagery from John's Gospel—"One of them, the disciple whom Jesus loved, was reclining next to Him. Simon Peter motioned to this disciple and said, 'Ask him which one he means.' Leaning back against Jesus, he asked Him, 'Lord, who is it?'" (John 13:23–25 NIV). Oh, that we all would be lovers of God, seated near Christ in the private place reserved for us, that we could so confidently declare of ourselves, as John did, that we are "the disciple whom Jesus loves." Before telling us what to do, Jesus tells us who we are. Everything good must flow out of a living relationship with Jesus. Our kingdom identity is formed as His heart is transferred to us.

REFLECTIONS

1. It's an inescapable reality of leadership that we'll always imitate the revolutionary we most admire. In other words, as leaders, patterning ourselves and our ministries after the purpose and personality of Jesus is the only way to ensure what we're building is the same as what He built. What are some ways you can spot an imposter? How can you make sure you aren't going astray?

2. If we settle for imitating only Christ's purpose, we can easily be misled by a leader's charisma and passion, their gifts and performance. It's how instead of following the Shepherd on the middle cross, we end up being led by a hired hand who may look the part of Christ but lacks the heart of Christ. What are some red flags to look for to keep you from following a hired hand?

3. When you read the portion on wounded shepherds, were you at all surprised? What specific information shared there stood out in particular for you? I sincerely hope you pray for your pastor because there's a very real enemy who desires to prey on your pastor. Besides prayer, what are some things that we in the body of Christ can do to help our leaders receive healing and accountability in an atmosphere of trust and transparency? How can they guard against isolation?

4. The kind of life and ministry modeled by Jesus (diakonia) is the only kind that counts. It's the only one that He'll bless, and it's the only way we can win the world. The disciples Christ came to make are humble servants, motivated by divine love. We often hear lip service paid to this kind of servant leadership, but how often have you actually seen it modeled up close? How have we

in the Western world settled for a suitable church when God intended it to be supernatural?

5. God calls us to seek first, not to serve first. If our doing doesn't flow out of our sense of being, then we end up offering something we ourselves don't possess. Do you feel like this order of priorities is what's reflected in church as you've experienced it? If not, why do you think that is?

C H A P T E R 4

THE COCKTAIL

Matthew and Mark both record that at Golgotha, Jesus was offered
a drink of wine drugged with myrrh or gall. Scholars have suggested
this cocktail of sorts was offered as an act of mercy, perhaps by local
Jewish women, to dull the pain. As prophesied in Psalms 69:19–21
(NIV), Jesus refused to drink this once He tasted the bitterness and
realized what it was. He would instead choose to remain in full
control of His mind, and under the full agony of His body, for the
entirety of the crucifixion process.

At the heart of Christian ministry, of course, is the message
of the cross—the gruesome story of Jesus laying down His life as
the perfect sacrifice to take away the sin of the world. The wine is
a representation of Christ's blood as we partake of communion in
remembrance of Him. We're entrusted with the sacred message of
this wine that has the power to produce a sweetness in our lives and
those we minister to. It's only by the blood that we're cleansed, set
free, and declared righteous. It's only by the blood that we can lay
claim to the precious promises of God in His Word. Yet with good
intentions, we too can be tempted to mix some things in to make it
easier on people. But in reality, the cocktail we've created hasn't just
dulled the pain, it's diminished the power.

Jesus was crucified at the time when Passover lambs would be slaughtered to commemorate this very special time of remembrance in Jewish tradition. In Exodus 12, the Israelites were commanded to kill a lamb and dip a branch of hyssop into its blood (Exodus 12:22 NLT). They were then to sprinkle the blood on the lintel and side posts of their front doors. That night, as the death angel came, God caused him to pass over every door where there was blood on the doorposts. Everyone whose doorposts had no blood lost their firstborn; those with the blood were spared. If an Israelite had left the blood in the basin instead of applying it, the death angel would've struck their home. Killing the lamb would have done them no good. The shedding of blood was not enough. The blood could only save them when it was taken out of the basin and applied.

Passover, of course, was a prophetic foreshadowing of the coming salvation of the Lord—of the perfect, spotless Lamb who would become the once-and-for-all sacrifice to atone for all humanity. This had always been the plan of God to redeem a world otherwise subjected to wrath and judgment. As Jesus rode into Jerusalem on Palm Sunday, He wept because He saw a religious people who shouted about salvation but refused to have the blood applied to their lives. This is why on the future day of judgment, people will be able to call Jesus "Lord" and still not be allowed to enter God's holy heaven (Matthew 7:21–23 NLT). People may place their hope in their love of God, their devotion to follow rules or practice religion, but if they don't have the blood applied, it won't be enough to keep the destroyer from coming and issuing judgment upon them. Any human effort to cover themselves will be completely futile.

No gift God has given us is more important than the blood of Jesus Christ. Yet many Christians don't fully comprehend the power of the blood. What's worse is that many churches, even whole denominations, have stopped preaching and singing about the blood and its power, presumably because its message is offensive to the rebellious and unrepentant. But what ability do we have to be saved apart from the blood? What hope is there for humanity without the message of pure wine that hasn't been mixed with the bitter myrrh or gall of our well-intentioned mercies? Our message must not be one that merely dulls the pain of the suffering. We must preach the whole counsel of scripture so that people can be saved—washed by the blood that gives men the right to boldly enter into this new covenant with God (Hebrews 10:19–22 NLT).

Before following the call of God into pastoral ministry, I had a fifteen-year career in social work. During my time in that field, I held a variety of positions that gave me a heart of compassion for the many hurting people I encountered. Early on, I'd been hired as a supervisor in a residential treatment facility for juveniles. One evening, while I was standing in the nurse's station eating my dinner, I was assaulted from behind by one of the juvenile residents—a violent seventeen-year-old man-child with a lengthy criminal record. While it wasn't uncommon for staff members to be the target of a resident's rage, the punch I took to the back of the head that day was one of the most severe I'd experienced. I remember seeing stars and feeling the surge of adrenaline coursing through my body. Ultimately recusing myself from the situation, I recall the relief I felt afterward because I'd maintained my professionalism and hadn't reacted hastily.

Later, I'd recommend to management and the clinical team that this young man's actions be reported to his probation officer, as his conduct seemed to only be getting worse—tormenting staff and residents alike, finding entertainment in the chaos he would cause, and depriving others of the treatment they were there to receive. Ultimately, management declined to report the incident, saying they thought it best to maintain the young man at their facility because they felt it was in his best interest. I'm sure the hefty per diem they were receiving from the state in exchange for their highest level of secure care had no bearing on their decision at all! Needless to say, it wasn't long after this incident that I would leave to work in a safer environment where juvenile delinquents weren't allowed to run the place.

While I'd love to say that social work is a profession with pure and selfless motives, I've had far too many experiences that have opened my eyes to the reality that there's a mixture involved. There are dueling motivations at play, some for the betterment of others and some for the betterment of self. I'm not trying to cast dispersions on social workers or the field in which they work. I know many wonderful people who've given their lives to helping others in this way, and I'm thankful for what they do. Sadly, however, I've come to realize that the church can often fall into a similar state—mixing the pure with the impure, its leaders having convinced themselves it's for the best, but this mixture comes with a hefty price tag.

Afraid to take a firm stand, caving to the pressure of popular opinion, and watering down the pure Gospel message of repentance for one that's more palatable, pastors operating in the fear of man have stopped preaching against sin, and many in our congregations are steeped in compromise. According to the Barna Research Group, the rate of divorce within the church is practically identical to that of the world (one in three). A national survey commissioned by Care Net indicates that four out of ten women who've had an abortion attended church at least once a month. And Pew Research Center reports only 50 percent of Evangelical Christians believe in absolute standards for right and wrong. I believe the church is entering one of the greatest harvest seasons we've ever seen, but if we're too busy playing church, we'll miss the moment. What the church of Jesus Christ needs in this hour isn't a more relevant approach, more attractive auditoriums and atmospheres, or better coffee bars. The church isn't an audience to be entertained; it's an army to be empowered. What we need is a fresh encounter with holiness that causes us to be distinct from the world, so we can once again offer them a pure Gospel that's strong enough to deliver them from the enemy's grip.

Eighteen years after being assaulted by that juvenile resident from Gary, Indiana, I still remember his name, and I can still picture his face. Out of curiosity, I conducted a criminal records search to see what his legal involvement had been since I last saw him, and it revealed a lengthy history of repeated battery, criminal confinement, domestic violence, and strangulation as recent as 2019. I was sad to see his life hadn't changed course and that he'd victimized so many more people over the years. I can only wonder how the trajectory of his life may have changed had the adults responsible for his care and discipline held him more accountable when he was young. A broken system just continues to produce broken people.

Tragic as this is, what should weigh heavier still on our hearts are the broken products of a broken church. How many people pass through its doors in need of radical, life-transforming truth, only to instead be given a feel-good message? How many have come in need of discipleship but instead have been met with entertainment? Jesus's discipleship plan started out with a message of "come and see" (John 1:39 NLT), but it ultimately led to one of "come and die" (Matthew 16:24 NLT). Making disciples is about transforming spectators into Christ imitators. If we fail to do this, none of our slick marketing, clever messaging, or good intentions will matter. All we will have managed to do is serve dying people a cocktail that numbs their pain but doesn't actually give them life. In this critical hour, the Lord's calling His church to repent of this unholy mixture and return to the place of holy awe that would make compromise unthinkable.

In the words of A.W. Tozer, "Our most pressing obligation today is to do all in our power to obtain a revival that will result in a reformed, revitalized, purified church. It is of far greater importance that we have *better* Christians than that we have *more* of them." Every great move of God in the earth is birthed through a leader who knows God deeply. Every movement of God in the earth is ended when the leader becomes the only one the followers know deeply. Leaders, we must go deep with God—not just deep intellectually or theologically but relationally. We must also take others with us, so they can be rooted in Christ, drawing from the source of living water for themselves. If we are to make strong, mature disciples, their primary attachment must be to the Lord Jesus Himself. Our goal must be that they become dependent on Him, independent of us, for He alone can purge our heart of the selfishness that's content in going to heaven by ourselves.

In his first letter to the church at Corinth, the apostle Paul writes that the message of the cross is foolishness to the world—worthless and confounding. Yet he also hails it as higher intelligence, superior wisdom, and the very power of God that produces our salvation (1 Corinthians 1:18, 27–28 NIV). Paul was a wise and educated man. While he was still fairly young, he was sent to Jerusalem to receive his education at the school of Gamaliel, one of the most noted teachers of Jewish law in history. In his natural abilities, Paul could have impressed his audiences with profound pontifications and reasoned with them through the powers of persuasion. But Paul made the decision early on that he wouldn't mix the pure with the impure. He wouldn't settle for the wisdom of man, but instead he would pursue the wisdom of God. Deciding to "forget everything except Jesus Christ, the one who was crucified," Paul relied only on the Holy Spirit to give him the words to say (1 Corinthians 2:2–5 NLT).

Today, have we traded the wisdom of God that makes us look like fools in the eyes of the world for the wisdom of man, thinking it will gain us respect in their eyes? May we be reminded today that like Jesus and Paul after Him, we aren't called to cater to the opinions of man—we're called to serve the will of God. May we not reduce our life and calling in order to accommodate our fears. May we not mix the pure with the impure, the potent with the impotent, and the ways of God with the ways of this world. The precious blood of Jesus—the pure wine of God poured out for sinful man—is far too valuable to be cheapened by the myrrh and gall of our good intentions. What God has in mind if far greater than we can imagine!

We were designed to live a powerful story of impossibilities made possible with a heavenly vision for our lives in partnership with the Holy Spirit. We mustn't settle for an impotent Gospel that's filled with words without wonder, doctrine without demonstration, and gatherings without glory. The greatest tragedy for the church of Jesus Christ is that we would become so watered down by the carnal ways of man that our lives and ministries would become easily explainable—devoid of power and flavorless to a world in desperate need to taste of the goodness of God. Shouldn't we at least wonder if the reason we aren't experiencing revival isn't just that we don't allow God to move enough but that we allow ourselves to move too much?

I submit that to regain the potency of the Gospel, we must get back to the way of the early believers who enjoyed the anointed preaching of the likes of Peter, John, Stephen, Phillip, and Paul and yet still prayed fervently for God to stretch forth His hand—that miracles, signs, and wonders would accompany the preaching of their message (Acts 4:29–31 NLT). Though they had more immediate and compelling evidence of the truth of the resurrection than any generation to follow, they embraced the reality that human hearts desperately needed to be struck with the awe and mystery of a supernatural move of God. We still need an unveiled Gospel (2 Corinthians 4:3 NIV) not only to be taught but to be *demonstrated*. Exhortation without example will never result in the kind of exceptional church we see in the New Testament. We need the pure, unmixed power of the Holy Spirit to bring the culture of heaven down to earth.

Revival is quite possibly one of the most misunderstood concepts in the church today. It's been seen as a formula to follow, a denominational doctrine, or the religious genre of a previous generation. Some have dubbed it emotionalism. Others have relegated it to an evening event. But the reality is that revival is the result of God breathing divine life into dead hearts and atmospheres, producing the revelation of what the normal Christian life is meant to look like. The radiant beauty of Christ's bride will be restored through revival. Anything less simply won't do. It's not about the methods of a bygone era. It's not about a style of preaching, a moment of church growth, a weeklong tent meeting, or an increase in spiritual manifestations. It's about becoming so desperate for the resurrected Son that we abandon every other strategy and focus the pursuit of our lives toward Him. It's about rejecting selfish living, greedy worship, fleshly prayer, and carnal pursuit to fix our gaze toward the only one who's worthy.

According to a study by Barna Research Group (Faith & Christianity in Millennials & Generations—September 4, 2019), the percentage of teens raised in church who walk away in their twenties is now 64 percent. Currently, one in four Americans consider themselves a practicing Christian—a number that's been cut in half since 2000. For the sake of a lost and dying world, we need revival! We can't afford to treat it as optional for one moment longer. God satisfies the hungry, He doesn't force-feed the satisfied. Throughout the history of the world, it's been the God-hungry men and women that heaven has worked through mightily to birth movements in the earth that send out waves to impact generations. This same God continues to search the earth for sons and daughters with an appetite for heaven to invade. And when it does, I assure you that the sound and appearance will be different from previous moves of God, but one constant we can count on is that the oil still works. The anointing is still strong enough to break every chain and destroy every yoke. This generation needs living epistles to display the power and love of Jesus.

When we preach Jesus, pursue Jesus, are passionate about Jesus, press into the person of Jesus, and rely on the power of Jesus, guess what? Jesus comes, and when He comes, everything we've attributed to revival comes with Him. See, revival doesn't heal the sick; Jesus does. Revival doesn't save the lost; Jesus does. Revival doesn't awaken the apathetic; Jesus does. Revival doesn't grow the church; Jesus does. Revival doesn't change cities; Jesus does. Revival doesn't drive out demons; Jesus does. Seeking revival isn't what'll bring revival. The Lord goes where He's wanted, and revival is the result of seeking Jesus. But as we see from the cautionary example found in Mark 6:1–6 (NLT), the quickest way to get Jesus to leave is to act like it's no big deal when He comes, and sadly, "in and out in an hour" has become the great commandment many churches now follow for their weekly services. So, as it was in Bethlehem, so it is in far too many Sunday-morning gatherings today—there's simply no room for Jesus.

Gone are the altar calls, prayer services, and tent revivals. Gone are the Sunday nights, midweek gatherings, and Sunday school. We must ask the question: how is it that we can offer less but somehow expect to get more? The reality is that one day, we'll all be gathered around the throne of God in heaven, joining our worship with the angels in perpetually declaring His majesty and worth. That fact isn't in dispute, but the truth is we're living as if our chief purpose is simply to get to heaven when Jesus made clear it's our job to bring heaven down to earth (Matthew 6:10, John 14:12 NLT). So if the cry of heaven is "Holy, holy, holy!" then the cry of the church mustn't be "Hurry, hurry, hurry!" We must understand the reality that's always been and will always be—that revival will pour out when we press in. Filled-up sanctuaries won't lead us into revival if prayer rooms remain empty. We must engage heaven in an Acts 2 kind of way if we're going to transform earth with an Acts 2 kind of power.

In the words of Smith Wigglesworth, "Pentecost came with the sound of a mighty rushing wind, a violent blast from heaven! Heaven has not exhausted its blasts, but our danger is we are getting frightened of them." And more specifically, what some church leaders are fearful of is how people might react if their church actually operated with the kind of power we read about in the New Testament. It's as if they think that a pure, unmixed move of God would shutter their doors and implode their ministry, and nothing could be more ludicrous. To be clear, revival will inevitably prune and purge, but the end result of God's fire upon His people isn't to weaken us but to strengthen our faith and resolve. Throughout history, revival has always served to propel the church forward in the face of poverty, persecution, martyrdom, wars, and injustice.

What the church has done for over two thousand years is what the church will continue to do; she'll thrive because the words of our King Jesus will continue to resound for many generations until His return—"I will build my Church and all the powers of hell will not conquer it" (Matthew 16:18 NLT). The only way we can fail is to dilute the pure, unmixed power of God to make it more palatable to people—to build something of our own invention that no longer bears much resemblance to the powerful church we read about that miraculously revolutionized the world. Such a watered-down gospel can only produce congregations of compromise who claim to know Jesus but at the judgment will only hear from Him the dreadful words of Matthew 7:23 (ESV), "I never knew you; depart from me." See, the reality of earth is that there are many churches, but heaven sees just one, the singular bride of Christ who's alive in Him, passionate about His presence, and lovesick for His return—that's who He's coming back to receive. So may we seek Jesus now with greater fervor than ever before. May our hearts be set ablaze as we run through fields of harvest with contagious wildfire. And may what some call a post-Christian civilization instead prove to be a pre-revival generation filled with divine purpose and potential.

REFLECTIONS

1. Paul made the decision early on that he wouldn't mix the pure with the impure. He wouldn't settle for the wisdom of man, but instead he would pursue the wisdom of God. Today, have we traded the wisdom of God that makes us look like fools in the eyes of the world for the wisdom of man, thinking it will gain us respect in their eyes? What are some examples of this that you've seen? Do you recognize in yourself the tendency, at times, to settle for living by man's wisdom?

2. One of the greatest tragedies for the church of Jesus Christ is that our lives and ministries have often become easily explainable—devoid of power and lacking in flavor. In our striving to become relevant, do you think the church has somehow lost its way, becoming an importer of (worldly) culture, rather than an exporter of (kingdom) culture? Take a few minutes and come up with a list of the church's cultural imports and exports. How does your list compare with how the early church operated in terms of the culture's effect on them and their effect on culture?

3. Read Acts 2:1–4. What was the role and result of the breath (Hebrew–"*ruach*") of God?

4. Ruach produces revival, and revival produces the revelation of what the normal Christian life is meant to look like. But the truth is revival is generally inconvenient, and it comes at great personal cost. Revival is agonizing because it so convicts you over your sin that you repent deeply. Revival is consuming, demanding your full attention, leaving little to no time for hobbies, television, or chores around the house. But ultimately,

it's God-hungry men and women who find God. When you examine the priorities of your life, what's revealed about your hunger? What about your church? If your prayers were answered and revival resulted, what would need to change about how you structure your schedule? Why not begin making those changes now in anticipation of what God might do? Could it be that God is waiting on you to shift your hunger and position yourself for the outpouring, so you'll be able to sustain the next revival He starts?

CHAPTER 5

THE ABUSES

As we walk through redemptive history, we see many explicit types and shadows of Christ. The Greek word *týpos*, meaning "type," describes a model or pattern in the Old Testament that's later fulfilled in the person of Jesus. When the light of Christ shines upon such a type, that type projects a shadow that bears resemblance to Jesus and serves as an extension of His divine nature in the natural world. Arguably, the clearest type given is that of David, a shepherd from Bethlehem chosen by God to be king of Israel. In 1 Samuel 17, we read the famous account of David's battle with the giant warrior from Gath, named Goliath. Hurling insults and abuses intended to taunt the armies of Israel and mock the God they served, he had the people cowering in fear and running for their lives. One of my favorite lines in the entire Bible has to be David's reply when this ogre tried cursing and threatening him in the same way. Just before running toward the Philistine champion and striking him with a stone to the forehead, David declares, "Today the Lord will conquer you, and I will kill you and cut off your head. And then I will give the dead bodies of your men to the birds and wild animals, and the whole world will know that there is a God in Israel!" (1 Samuel 17:46 NLT). Now that's the type of king I can get behind!

So when Jesus was hanging on the cross at Golgotha and the

leading priests, the teachers of religious law, and the elders began to mock Him (Matthew 27:41 NLT), hurling abuses at the King of kings, one might expect that He'd have an equally sharp comeback that let these hypocrites know He was fixin' to knock their teeth so far down their throat they'd spit 'em out in single file. And He certainly had the ability to do it! Yet Christ would willingly endure the abuses, being taunted and teased by Jew and Gentile alike, with the Roman soldiers and even the other revolutionaries being crucified with Him piling on. Just as the prophet Isaiah had foretold, like a sheep being led to the slaughter or a lamb that's silent before its shearers, Jesus didn't open His mouth (Isaiah 53:7 NIV). While Paul says in Galatians 6:7 (KJV) that "God is not mocked," this is precisely because God had been mocked, and at Golgotha, Jesus was content to just let them figure out the truth three days later.

It's been said that a lie can travel halfway around the world while the truth is still putting on its shoes, and any leader who's been in their role for longer than five minutes can probably relate. There is perhaps no greater test of a leader's character and resolve than when their name is slandered and their patience is tested. How easy it would be for someone armed with the truth and a microphone to filet someone open in retaliation. What quick work it would be for a minister to avenge a wrong by betraying a confidence, or to clean up their reputation by muddying up another's. And how often it's happened! In leadership, you have to make tough calls, and inherently, you will run the risk of being misunderstood. Ultimately, however, we're not in the reputation management business. We're in the laying down our lives business, and when we do that as Christ did, we'll endure the same things He endured. If we haven't made peace with that fact, then the reality is we've not counted the cost and should probably just quit and go sell ice cream because the need to be liked will never be satisfied in ministering the Gospel.

In Acts 5 (NLT), we see this incredible account of the apostles performing numerous miracles, signs, and wonders in the name of Jesus. Crowds were coming and being saved, healed, and delivered as the Good News was preached. Sick people were even being laid in the streets on beds and mats so Peter's shadow could fall across them as he went by. Revival was in full swing, and the power of the Holy Spirit was on full display. Not everyone was a fan though, so it wasn't long before the apostles faced fierce opposition from the high priest and Sadducees who were filled with jealousy. Arrested and imprisoned, Peter and the boys had a decision to make then and there—either they would fear man and manage their reputation, or they would fear God and simply let their shadow speak.

When we stop to consider the light of Christ that shone upon Peter's life and the radiant witness he was for the Lord, isn't it only fitting that his shadow would carry so much power? Peter didn't consider it pride to say that he had power from God. Rather, love compelled him to project the healing nature of the Savior into a world filled with hurting people. Like Peter, Jesus also didn't feel the need to defend Himself because His shadow spoke loudly of His compassion, character, and fruitfulness. As followers of Christ then, we must ask ourselves what message our shadow is communicating and whose nature it's reflecting. When we're being attacked or wrongly accused, could it be that the enemy sees divine potential in our shadow that we don't? On the other hand, when we feel the need to defend ourselves, rather than simply letting our shadow speak, could it be we aren't content with what it would say?

Had Jesus not endured the abuses on the cross, the apostles may have been convinced that the rejection they faced from religious leaders was an indictment on their leadership. But the truth is that healthy and mature leaders must learn to absorb pain without passing it down to those they lead. See, God will often use the trials you face as a training ground to build your character, so you can sustain your calling. Like with David, God may allow a Saul in your life to teach you how not to treat people when He promotes you. Like with Paul, God may allow a thorn in your flesh to teach you that your inadequacies and limitations are actually gifts that help to keep you humble and connected. And like with Peter, God may allow the critics in your life to teach you that the call of God isn't dependent on the approval of man. They may not understand or support the call you received, and that's okay because it wasn't a conference call. So you really don't need them to! What you need is to listen to the voice of the one who called you more than you listen to the voice of your insecurities that seek to limit your leadership potential. Don't give in to Satan's scheme to lure you into defending a reputation you've already crucified.

Wherever the Gospel is being preached and the Spirit of God is moving, the enemy will mount opposition. Anyplace where heaven is invading earth, hell is going to wage war, and it will often come through religious people because the spirit of religion has targeted the ministry of the Holy Spirit as enemy number one. By means of control and intimidation, those who desire the pleasures of man more than the pleasures of God will do everything in their power to choke out the spontaneous, unscripted move of the Spirit in the name of either reverence or relevance. However, don't be misled by what may seem on the surface to be noble intentions. At the heart of this demonic agenda is an unholy spirit that seeks to upend a move of God so that supernatural shadows have no chance of being cast on people in the streets. The enemy will do everything he can to thwart a move of God, and if he can't stop it dead in its tracks, he'll settle for containing it to the four walls of the church building, where its impact will be limited and short-lived.

Prior to the crucifixion, Luke's Gospel records a separate account of Jesus enduring verbal abuses during His trial. Here we read that "Herod was delighted at the opportunity to see Jesus, because he had heard about Him and had been hoping for a long time to see Him perform a miracle. He asked Jesus question after question, but Jesus refused to answer. Meanwhile, the leading priests and the teachers of religious law stood there shouting their accusations. Then Herod and his soldiers began mocking and ridiculing Jesus. Finally, they put a royal robe on Him and sent Him back to Pilate" (Luke 23:8–11 NLT). Then we read in the parentheses this very interesting sentence: "Herod and Pilate, who had been enemies before, became friends that day" (Luke 23:12 NLT). What a powerful picture of how unity works! See, there's a holy unity where we're united to fellow believers by our mutual love for Jesus, but there's also an unholy unity where we become united in our offense. Make no mistake, a spirit of offense is one of the primary weapons Satan uses against the church today because he understands that what it takes to offend you is all it takes to defeat you. This is why it's so vital that we work to protect the unity among believers and strive to be peacemakers wherever the enemy tries to bring strife.

Concerning the great danger of offense threatening the church, the apostle Paul sends stern warning to the Ephesian believers, saying, "Do not grieve the Holy Spirit of God, with whom you were sealed for the day of redemption. Get rid of *all* bitterness, rage and anger, brawling and slander, along with every form of malice. Be kind and compassionate to one another, forgiving each other, just as in Christ God forgave you" (Ephesians 4:30–32 NIV). As Christians, it's absolutely essential that we understand the sensitivity of the Holy Spirit—that the offenses we hold onto and the bitterness or unforgiveness that we harbor grieves Him and separates us from His abiding presence, attracting death and destruction in our lives and in our ministries. The writer of Hebrews puts it this way: "Make every effort to live in peace with everyone and to be holy; without holiness no one will see the Lord. See to it that no one falls short of the grace of God and that no bitter root grows up to cause trouble and defile many" (Hebrews 12:14–15 NIV).

Bitterness and unforgiveness function as a spiritual and relational cancer that cannot be contained. Scripture is clear that it absolutely will spread, and the result is that it will defile many. There's actually a theme in the Bible that connects demonic activity with the sin of unforgiveness, saying in 2 Corinthians 2 that we must forgive so that we aren't outwitted by the devil's schemes. James says that bitter people are earthly, unspiritual, and demonic (James 3:15 NLT). If we let the sun go down on our anger, the Bible says we give the devil a foothold (Ephesians 4:26–27 NLT). The connection between unforgiveness and demonic activity exists because hell is the place of unforgiveness where nobody is forgiven. Heaven is the place of forgiveness where everyone is forgiven. So here in the middle on earth, when we forgive, we pull heaven down into our circumstances. And when we choose not to forgive, we pull hell up into our lives. We cannot expect the *Holy* Spirit to dwell in our lives when we are welcoming in *unholy* spirits through unforgiveness.

Bitterness left unchecked in our lives will ultimately defile us and everyone under our influence. The truth is we can only impart wholeness to the extent that we ourselves are whole. Unforgiveness then limits our ability to produce healthy disciples and cultivate healthy environments. Therefore, if we harbor the offense, it becomes inevitable that we will inadvertently reproduce toxicity in what we touch. While this seems to be such an obvious leadership pitfall to avoid, the reason it often flies below our radar is that bitterness is always justifiable to the bitter. Satan knows that a lie won't be perceived as a lie if we'll hear it in our own voice. So, if we have a "good enough" reason, we'll hang onto the things that are holding us back. If we want to walk in complete freedom and lead people likewise, we have to stop allowing bitterness to rob us with our agreement.

If we're not careful to guard our hearts, Jesus teaches that we can become so offended that we start to hate the very people Jesus loved enough to die for (Matthew 24:10–13 NLT). Offense at the sins of others is sometimes even more damaging than the sin itself. It opens us up to an opposite spirit that turns our hearts away from God's mercy, turning our wounds into weapons and us into accusers of our fellow man. To embrace offense is to invite deception that blinds us to our own faults and drives us toward the bondage of hate. Offense will steal your peace and freedom, so remain vigilant in opposing every hint of it in your life. A healed person who acts from their heart will always produce life, but a bitter person who acts from their pain will only reproduce death. Healing is how we stop the wounding from being repeated. The calling that lies in front of you is far greater than the offenses that lie behind you. So vow to be better than what broke you. Be healed and determine that the enemy's hold on your heart ends here and now!

As leaders, not only do we need to examine what has a grip on our hearts, but we must also be discerning and wise about who we yoke ourselves to. We need to be on guard against the cunning agenda of the enemy, who will often send in a counterfeit apostle that will cozy up to leadership for personal gain. So long as they hold a position of authority and they're getting something out of the relationship, they'll tend to go undetected. But when either their control is challenged or they're required to pay a price, the true nature of this Judas spirit is exposed. Desiring intimacy without covenant, betrayal comes easily to someone with a nature like this, because although they cohabitate with the bride of Christ, they aren't really legitimate fathers. They're merely in a relationship of convenience, and when the bride refuses to allow the abuses to continue, these people have no problem leveraging relationship to manipulate others into taking sides, tearing apart the family and leaving a wake of destruction in their path. Forgiving such a person is essential to your freedom. Entrusting positions of influence and leadership to them, however, is a surefire way to welcome in disunity and destruction.

While many in the church are hyperalert to potential threats posed by the outside world, a true shepherd of the flock knows to be on guard for wolves in sheep's clothing who will threaten from *within* the sheepfold. To guard against this danger, leaders would be wise to align themselves with people who are talent rich but ego poor—those who have gifts to offer but have no guile in their heart, no interest in building a name for themselves. Faithfulness to serve God in ministry and loyalty to honor and protect one's leadership must accompany fruitfulness for the kingdom. A true shepherd recognizes the inherent risk associated with elevating a person to a place of influence that's beyond what their integrity can support, and refuses to amplify the voice of those who would use their platform to verbally abuse those they dislike or disagree with. Yoking ourselves or our ministries to people like this has the potential to stunt growth and choke out life because we become yoked up not only with a person but with the spiritual stronghold of offense, discouragement, or rebellion that's attached itself to them. It's time that we destroy any unholy union that compromises our effectiveness and exercise the authority that's ours to tear down enemy strongholds in order to propel God's purposes forward in the earth and create safe places for people to find freedom.

If you're facing opposition today and the abuses seem to be flying fast and furious in your direction, be encouraged that while you may be praying for God to get you out of a situation, He has plans to bring you through. You weren't called to cut your losses and run; you were called to persevere in Jesus and contend for the value that's found on the other side of victory. It'll take boldness and radical faith on your part, but with your eyes fixed on the promises God has in store, you can be assured that today's trials will become tomorrow's treasures. When you feel overwhelmed and you can't see a way out, God sees through to the other side. Where you see only opposition, God sees opportunity. Serve faithfully, pray fervently, and begin looking at your situation through God's eyes. Don't listen to enemy voices set out to distract and discourage you. Remember, the most dangerous you is the you that believes what God says! So leave your reputation in His hands and simply let your shadow speak.

When I think back on the times in my life and ministry when I faced my greatest opposition and endured the ugliest abuses from my critics, I'll never forget the best advice I received, and it was simply to laugh! At first, it sounded ludicrous, and I honestly questioned the person's sanity a little when they said it. But as they spoke with grace and clarity, having walked through the fire themselves, I realized the power of partnering with the sound of heaven over my situation. Just listen to the words of the psalmist, David who wrote, "The wicked plot against the godly; they snarl at them in defiance. But the Lord just laughs, for He sees their day of judgment coming" (Psalm 37:12–13 NLT). David was now old when he penned these words, having learned that God directs the steps of the godly, that He holds their hand and will never abandon them (Psalm 37:23–25 NLT). We can laugh with confidence because what looks like a setback now will be revealed as a setup in the end. Our natural reaction to opposition is often to worry and fret, but don't give wickedness the power to rule your heart through fear and intimidation. May there be no space between heaven and your heart, such that the laughter of the Lord would be louder in your ear than the snarl of the enemy. Let supernatural joy flood your soul so you can laugh at the foolishness of the enemy and celebrate in advance what God's getting ready to do!

Be encouraged that the adversity you face in one season can be used by God as the source of your stability in the next. Sometimes the only thing necessary to win the battle is to determine you're going to outlast your enemy. Like a mighty oak tree that thrives in the midst of drought and storm, if you respond to the difficulty by sending your roots down deeper in Jesus, you'll find that even the greatest tests and trials won't be able to affect your ability to bear fruit. Your life will be an evidence that through Christ, hurt doesn't have to harm, and purpose can be produced from pain. In the hands of the Lord, the weapons formed against you will become the tools used to shape you. And the end result will be that you become for others what you wish someone had been for you—a place of shade to cover the hurting, a source of nourishment to sustain the weary, and a pillar of strength to stabilize the broken.

As the apostle Paul wrote to the church at Corinth, God "comforts us in all our troubles so that we can comfort others. When they are troubled, we will be able to give them the same comfort God has given us" (2 Corinthians 1:4 NLT). See, the abuses Jesus suffered on the cross and the abuses we suffer in following Him aren't without purpose. And it's better to hurt with a purpose than to exist without one. To suffer with Christ is to partner with

God in planting more great oaks (Isaiah 61:3 NLT), multiplying the life-giving effects of Golgotha's tree and producing a harvest of righteousness for His namesake. This is the Gospel method by which we'll be able to pass something of immeasurable value to the next generation, so that what isn't completed by us will be completed by our legacy. So don't grow weary in your well doing today because a great harvest awaits if you don't give up!

REFLECTIONS

1. Like Peter, when the light of Christ and His nature shines upon our lives, we cast a shadow that communicates Christlike character and fruitfulness. Satan sees into the divine potential that we carry, even when we don't. So we shouldn't be surprised when we're attacked or wrongly accused. As you reflect upon times in your life when you've experienced this, do you feel the need to defend yourself, or are you content with simply letting your shadow speak? Are you content with what it would say?

2. A spirit of offense is one of the primary weapons Satan uses against the church today, and if you see others' actions toward you through the lens of your pain or the lens of your pride, you'll inevitably end up offended. The enemy employs the weapon of offense because he understands that what it takes to offend you is all it'll take to defeat you. As you reflect on the times you've been offended by the abuses and criticisms of others, do you find that you viewed their actions through the lens of your pain or through the lens of your pride? Your answer to that question will determine what it'll take to remove offense at its root level. If it's pain, you need healing. If it's pride, you need humbling. Which one do you need to live free and avoid Satan's trap of offense?

3. The offenses we hold onto and the bitterness or unforgiveness that we harbor grieve the Holy Spirit and separate us from His abiding presence, attracting death and destruction in our lives and in our ministries. Bitterness and unforgiveness function as a spiritual and relational cancer that cannot be contained. We can't expect the Holy Spirit to dwell in our lives when we're

welcoming in unholy spirits through unforgiveness. Is there someone you need to forgive today?

4. The most dangerous you is the you that believes what God says. Take a moment and write down five things God says about you. Which of these is hardest for you to believe? What would change about you if you lived as though you truly believed each of these statements were true?

C H A P T E R 6

THE MOURNERS

The cross of Jesus Christ has been used and misused in a number of ways over the past two millennia. From the shields of the crusaders in medieval times to the jewelry of Madonna in music videos of the 1980s, and most disgustingly, the burning crosses of the Ku Klux Klan that surfaced in the early twentieth century, the cross has been hijacked by many people and groups with divisive and destructive purposes. For this reason, the secular world has largely attached slanderous stigmas to this sacred symbol. However, the first misuse of the cross wasn't done within medieval military, donned in music videos, or demonized by masked men. The first misuse of the cross was delivered in religious forms devoid of power that were chock-full of rules and regulations. Oh, how that cheapened its meaning and message in the eyes of men!

Again, to be clear, I write these things as a pastor who loves the church dearly and would never disparage or disgrace her. The church of Jesus Christ was God's idea, and its origins can be traced back to the cross at Golgotha where a group of mourners wept at the sight of the sinless Savior giving His life for hopeless sinners. The problem is that God's idea seems to have gotten lost somewhere along the way and has been replaced by our own. The words spoken by Christ to His followers at the cross are filled with incarnate intention. John records that "Standing near the cross were Jesus' mother, and His mother's sister, Mary (the wife of Clopas), and Mary Magdalene. When Jesus saw His mother standing there beside the disciple He loved, He said to her, 'Dear woman, here is your son.' And He said to this disciple, 'Here is your mother.' And from then on this disciple took her into his home" (John 19:25–27 NLT). What Golgotha makes clear is that Jesus didn't come to start a new religion; He came to form a new spiritual family.

The distinction between the two concepts is more than mere semantics and is worthy of our sober examination. If we call one another "brother" and "sister" but fail to love one another as Christ intended, we may have the wording right, but our actions are speaking so loudly, no one can hear what we're saying. If we've professionalized ministry for a few "qualified" titleholders in the church, rather than revolutionizing the world with an unlimited number of image bearers, our pews may be full, but our people have been emptied of purpose. If we have teams of staff to train up servants but lack spiritual mothers and fathers to raise up sons and daughters, we've settled for a corporate blueprint that has people climbing ladders of ambition instead of sitting at family tables where their hearts can be imprinted by heavenly affection.

As difficult as it may be for us, if we're to get back to being the family God intended for us to be, we must first assess our current condition and remove the things that stand in the way. Consumerism has to be one of the greatest roadblocks facing the American church today. With most congregations having 80 to 90 percent of the work being done by 10 to 20 percent of the people, there's little opportunity for others to grow in their gifts and callings unless the "professionals" are intentional about doing less. In order for this to be possible, the perfectionistic standards of performance have to give way to grace-filled opportunities for trial and error. It's the only way for more opportunities to be created, especially in a church climate where midweek gatherings are becoming less frequent and Sunday-night services are virtually extinct.

If we wait for people to simply measure up and meet our high standards, there'll always be someone for them to compare themselves to and easily conclude they're incapable because that someone could just do it better. I fear there are people who God wants to use as the imperfect vessels they are, and if we don't create opportunities for them to serve and minister in who God has made them to be, we will in effect rob them of their purpose and rob ourselves of their impact. It's time we dethrone the unrelenting idol of performance that's been used to attract people. Failing to do so means we'll have to continue to appease its demands if we want to keep the people coming. We must rid our hearts and God's house of all inferior lovers and shift our affection solely to the Father. The truth is that a church who genuinely values discipleship over performance will produce disciples, not performers. So why don't more churches place greater value on discipleship? I'd suggest two reasons. First, it requires much more work to make disciples than it does to train performers. And second, true discipleship involves leading others toward wholeness and healing in every area. Sadly, this is a journey many leaders haven't taken for themselves, and therefore, they're unable to lead the way in it.

How we define success and who we look to as models of effective ministry must change if we're going to hit the target of functioning as a biblical family. God intends to change the world through the local church, and at the last supper with His disciples, Jesus tells them exactly what they must do if they are to accomplish this purpose. He says, "Now I am giving you a new commandment: Love each other. Just as I have loved you, you should love each other. Your love for one another will prove to the world that you are my disciples" (John 13:34–35 NLT). So here Jesus gives us the *command*; He gives us the *key* to let the world know we've been sent by God. And what do we do? We create attractional models, aesthetically pleasing atmospheres, cool coffee shops, and slick advertising campaigns. Is it just me, or are we clearly telling Jesus that we think we know better than Him? It's no wonder we seem to have lost our way!

Until we learn to truly love one another as Christ commanded, I don't care how dynamic the speaker is, how beautiful the worship sounds, or how impressive the facilities look. We've tried all of those things. There are churches knocking it out of the park on all that stuff, but they're still not accomplishing what we read about the church doing in the New Testament. The hard truth is it doesn't matter how big or how nice the orphanage is. It doesn't matter how well it's run or how excellent the education that's provided. At the end of the day, nothing can replace the love and belonging only a family can provide. Without the nurturance of spiritual parents, the church may be filled with consumers and even produce converts, but it won't convince the world of Christ.

Do you think maybe it's time we finally just submit to doing things God's way? Maybe you think I'm exaggerating here. Well, let me echo a question posed by Francis Chan in his book *Letters to the Church* and ask you to make a list of the churches in your community that are known for how well they love one another. How about churches in America that are known for this? Out of approximately 380,000 churches in this nation, can you name even one that's operating in the kind of supernatural love and unity with one another that the church of the New Testament had? The fact that we even have to ask the question should tell us that we have a serious problem on our hands!

Love and unity work hand in hand and are two qualities that even unbelievers hold in high regard, and the world is utterly desperate for. There has quite possibly been no clearer evidence of this desperation in recent history than in the wake of the tragic and detestable killing of George Floyd in Minneapolis during the summer of 2020. While many may disagree over the politics involved or the riots that ensued, anyone who took time to step back from the polarizing rhetoric could clearly see the immense pain of humanity that emanated from a place of deep division and disunity. After a long series of horrific injustices perpetrated against black Americans and an inordinate number of young black lives cut short (though one is too many), communities across the nation were understandably weighed down by intense feelings of grief, fear, and outrage. Questions heavy on the hearts of the hurting included things like "Does my life matter to people who don't look like me?" "Will I ever be able to let my son or daughter drive down the street or go for a jog without having to fear for their safety?" and "Is justice only available to those Americans who were born into the majority in this country?"

On the day George Floyd's life was taken from him, like so many other people, I found myself staring at the screen in absolute shock and disbelief as the video of him lying on the street with a knee to his neck played over and over. This was a woman's son, a child's father, and a precious human being created in the image of God. Tears streaming down my face and fervent prayers overflowing from my soul with words intelligible only to the ear of heaven, I truly believed this could be the moment the church of Jesus Christ would stand boldly against hatred and injustice, united in a message of compassion and grace that would let the world come to know the divine love that dwells within us. This was an opportunity for heaven to invade earth as every tongue, tribe, and nation joined together as one family in a kind of supernatural unity that could only be possible in Jesus's name.

Yet in the aftermath of that unconscionable travesty, I learned just how out of touch I was with the state of our nation and the condition of the church. As one Christian friend after another sounded off on social media, slamming the sympathizers and maligning the merciful, I quickly realized that we as a people were still heartbreakingly divided over the value of a human being and chillingly complicit in the oppression of our black brothers and sisters. Now, you may read those words and find them difficult to stomach. You may wonder why we even need to talk about George Floyd or rehash the disunity and division that erupted that summer. Simply put, it never went away—some people just moved on and went back to burying their heads in the sand, pretending all is well in the church. But the fact is denying a problem's existence has never produced solutions, and doing so will only serve to further the divide among us.

If you find this to be a difficult subject for you, lean into that feeling. Ask yourself why you so quickly want to escape this conversation and look away from the pain. I challenge you to really listen to the voices of Christian brothers and sisters who look different from you and who are expressing a different viewpoint because the truth sometimes hurts, it always helps, and ultimately it heals. If all you want to know is more of what you already know, you're limiting and hindering your walk with God. As for my wife and I, we decided we couldn't look away in the midst of our family members (both natural and spiritual) suffering in anguish.

We heard that our alma mater was hosting the funeral for George Floyd, and we decided to make the drive up to stand out in the streets with thousands of others. We weren't there to make a statement; we were there to learn, to grow, and to change. As the sound of Gospel music played over the PA system, we lifted our hands in worship, and we were met by such a sweet presence of the Lord. We visited the third precinct, and what we saw were people caring for, praying for, and rooting for one another. It was truly a beautiful sight to behold—a far cry from the anarchy playing out in the media each night before. While several friends expressed concern for us, we knew this was a pilgrimage we needed to make, and what we experienced there impacted our hearts forever. Street evangelism was taking place. People were coming to Christ, being baptized in water, and pledging to be a part of the solution. I was so encouraged!

In the midst of all the chaos and turmoil, I received a series of messages from a fellow pastor who'd seen my statements on social media, voicing support for my black brothers and sisters. He asked, "Is this issue the hill that God has called you to plant your flag on and go to war on? Consider the audience where God has called you to minister." His argument being that ministry in a rural white culture was incompatible with advocacy for racial equality and that for me to do so was to risk alienating my community and congregation. I'd like to submit to you that this is at the root of the problem we're facing—people of position, privilege, and influence who are unwilling to risk their reputation unless they perceive some benefit to themselves in terms of advancing their own agenda. I let him know unequivocally that we will always plant our flag in the camp of the hurting, siding with the oppressed rather than the oppressor and using our voice to be an agent of healing. As the church of Jesus Christ, we must open our hearts to the reality of the Gospel that the enemy of our enemy is, in fact, our friend—worthy of our love, loyalty, and liberation. As the people of the cross, this is precisely what our lives are to be marked by.

Culture wars continue to rage today. Intense issues remain contentious and divisive. As I write this now, America is in a state of brokenness and disarray—confused, hurting, hurting each other, killing themselves, and killing one another. Gun violence is in the news on a daily basis, gas prices are at an all-time high, the economy seems to be on the verge of collapse with inflation soaring and stocks plummeting, and there's wicked rage being unleashed in response to the landmark ruling by the Supreme Court that overturned *Roe v. Wade*. Everything is incessantly politicized, and opinions are increasingly polarized. We can hardly catch our breath before yet another wave of news breaks, pitting people against one another in a no-holds-barred battle where allies are identified with virtue signaling and enemies are targeted by cancel culture.

Christians are constantly taking sides and getting sucked into the cacophony of voices reverberating over the sound waves and online. Meanwhile, the number one question that I believe needs to be answered is "Where is the church of Jesus Christ?" Not simply "What is our stance?" Not merely "Whose side are we on?" But when people are hurting, "Where are we?" Are we so busy rebuking oppression that we ignore the oppressed? Are we so preoccupied with the schemes of the enemy that we fail to take part in God's redemptive plan for humankind? Have we forgotten that although we're not of this world, Jesus sent us on mission here "to bring Good

News to the poor, to proclaim that captives will be released, that the blind will see, that the oppressed will be set free and that the time of the Lord's favor has come" (Luke 4:18–19 NLT)? The bottom line is that Jesus didn't come to win arguments. He came to win people. If we settle for winning the argument but lose relationship with people in the process, what is it we've won?

We can and should take a stand for righteousness. We can and should wage battle against the forces of darkness. But we can't fight for God using the devil's arsenal. We can't worship God as treasure while we treat people like trash. The ends are never justified if the means employed aren't Christlike. When we come to Jesus, we get more than a new iTunes playlist. We get an entirely new heart, but when the world looks upon our lives, is that apparent to them? See, the world needs more than to hear new songs—they need to be shown a new way! Are we known for the points we make with our lips or the difference we make with our lives? We should be reminded that Jesus turned up at far more tables than He turned over. And when He spent time with people who knew they were far from God, Jesus was tender with His judgments and aggressive with His mercies. May we never get it backward! Our compassion will always reach more people than our opinions.

In a culture where people are harshly judged, we need to let people know that they are fiercely loved. We cannot allow our witness to become weaponized, taking aim at human enemies. Wagging an angry, religious finger at the world and branding them as evil will never cause the lost to want to join the saved club. Jesus didn't come to rebuke them; He came to redeem them. Jesus made other people's problems His problems, and so should we. People need to know that the brokenness of this world can be healed, that their sins can be forgiven, and that their trials and struggles can be overcome. The apostle Paul tells us how we're to engage with one another as the family of God. He says, "Don't just pretend to love others. Really love them. Hate what is wrong. Hold tightly to what is good. Love each other with genuine affection, and take delight in honoring each other" (Romans 12:9–10 NLT). The unity of believers on earth echoes the agreement of heaven. It reveals a better way to be human that attracts the blessing of God. Whether an earthly audience approves or not, we must be eternally minded in our approach to humankind. We must live as citizens of heaven and messengers of Good News in a world being torn apart at the seams. A great cloud of witnesses surrounds us; we are being recorded in heaven's living saga!

My Jesus dined with sinners, and He died for sinners. Rather than yelling at them, He ate with them. He cracked the whip and flipped tables on the Pharisees and religious hypocrites. Still today, the Lord detests anything that would keep lost people from finding God. In order for the bride of Christ to become purified, she must first be purged of her pride. In order for the church to become the hospital for the hurting Jesus intended, it must first be delivered from its duplicity. In Matthew 5:43–48 (NLT), what Christ wants us to understand about living as true children of our Father in heaven is that our Christianity isn't most tested by how we love Jesus but rather by how we love Judas (our enemy and betrayer).

It's high time that the church in America be known by who we're for, rather than what we're against. A clear demonstration of Jesus must precede our preaching, and the only way for that to occur is for us to do away with the "us and them" mentality and become the family He commanded us to be—united in heart and committed to loving as Christ did. The enemy would have us to believe we're in a love/hate battle. But the truth is we're in a love/love battle. The devil loves sin, and God loves sinners. I believe when the church of Jesus Christ is able to love people more than those people love their sin, the devil doesn't stand a chance. Why? Because to know the love of God is to find Him irresistible!

In Luke 10 (NLT), Jesus tells the story of the Good Samaritan, where a man was robbed and left for dead, until a Samaritan passing by stopped to place him on a donkey and carry him to help. Now, we often make this story about helping others in need, but that really wasn't the point. See, to the people listening to Jesus, the Samaritans were the opposition. To them, there was no such thing as a *good* Samaritan because they believed there was nothing good about the Samaritans. Jesus told this parable while discussing a verse in the Hebrew Bible about loving your neighbor. Asked to define the meaning of "neighbor," Jesus told a story where the member of a despised people group was the "neighbor," making a Samaritan man (*the opposition*) the hero of the story!

Now, this isn't some woke theology or hippy "peace and love" message. Jesus's point was quite literally that we shouldn't just love our friends or the people who look like us, agree with us, and vote like us—but everyone! The Hebrew word we translate as "neighbor" in this verse is "rea" (רֵעַ), which can mean "friends" but can also be translated as "opponents." In other words, Jesus is teaching that our neighbors are even the people who are against us. Jesus sets a different example for His followers. And it harkens back to the two greatest commandments He gives—to love the Lord our God with all our heart, all our soul, all our mind, and all our strength and to love our neighbor as we love ourselves (Luke 10:27 NLT). This means caring for and being kind to people with opposing religious views, who weren't born where you were, who have a lifestyle you disagree with, and those voting for the other political candidate. It means identifying with another's suffering and extending mercy when mercy has been withheld from them. That's loving your neighbor. That's the Gospel according to Jesus.

We must be careful living in a secular society where politics turn into religion—where political rallies become worship services, campaigning becomes evangelism, and candidates become saviors. In this warped reality, loving your (political) enemies becomes an impossibility because they're perceived as demons to be exorcised instead of lost souls in need of saving. Christian, it's time to wake up to the reality that politics as religion will only disciple you into a person of hatred. If you identify with the title of conservative or progressive more than Christian, that's a problem because complete alignment with the kingdoms of earth is misalignment with the kingdom of God. We Christians in America sure seem to love us some culture wars though! As if contending for them is the same as contending for the Gospel of Christ. It's not. If our theology doesn't lead to a greater love of God and neighbor, we're seriously missing it! We must remind ourselves that Jesus didn't change the world by waging war against the Roman Empire or by vilifying Caesar. Instead, He ushered in an otherworldly kingdom that promoted humbling oneself to allow God to do the exalting. Similarly, the early church was radically effective not because they engaged in warring against the prevailing culture but because they were so good at cultivating kingdom culture marked by honor, humility, and holiness.

Our job isn't to throw stones. We're not in the business of finger pointing. We're in the business of snatching people from the flames. Guilt just produces more bondage. Grace is what actually sets people free. Enemies of the cross are not my enemies. They are victims of my enemy. My heart's desire must be for them to be free. The fact is that anyplace there's pain, heartache, and need, God lives there. And if God is near to such people and places, don't you think His people should be there also? Our job description is given to us in John 8:1–11 (NLT), and it's to lift the fallen, restore the broken, and heal the hurting. And all of our good intentions will ultimately amount to nothing if nothing materializes from them. People can't hear what we *meant* to say; it's the words we speak and the action to back up the talk that makes a difference. See, more than just building ministries, we're called to build people. Jesus builds His church, and His platform is our lives. Therefore, the message we preach to the world is only valid if we model the agape love of the Father to a broken and hurting world.

In Amos 5, God brings a rebuke against the temple worship being offered by the people because He takes issue with their duplicity. He warns of severe judgment that will come if they don't honor the desires of His heart. The Lord says, "Away with your noisy hymns of praise! I will not listen to the music of your harps. Instead, I want to see a mighty flood of justice, an endless river of righteous living" (Amos 5:23–24 NLT). Religious hypocrites often found themselves in the crosshairs of Jesus because He personified the Father's heart for justice, righteous living, and continuity between word and deed. See, the Good Samaritan story Jesus told isn't just an example of compassionate spirituality. It's a critique against religious passivity. The modern-day application being that if church people won't work for justice and mercy, God will find some other people who will. So be careful of the *other* you judge because they might just end up being the very ones God uses to carry out His purposes and reveal His heart to the world.

Courageous leaders have double vision. They see the world both as it is and as it could be, with hearts consumed by both the burden of the hurting and the hope of the Healer. The two are forged together by the fire of the Spirit, who both comforts and conquers. The Gospel holds the answers to the problems of this world, and the reality is that if the crucifixion of Jesus can be made beautiful, then there's no ugliness of the human condition that can't be redeemed by its beauty. Placing our faith in Christ's ability to redeem and restore all things means that *avoiding* evil isn't what following Jesus is about. It's about *overcoming* evil with the same love that not only overcame the evil in us but also brought forth resurrection life from our lifeless ashes. The only people in scripture who had a problem with this concept were the hypocritical religious leaders of the day who Jesus rebuked for being blind guides, leading others to fall into pits (Matthew 15:14 NIV). This tells me I can either be a person who looks for opportunities to redeem what's broken around me, or I can be offended with Jesus because His ways go against my religious rules. What I can't do is claim to follow Jesus while acting morally superior to Him and rejecting the very people He came to save!

Jesus desires for us to be a spiritual family, united in heart and purpose for His kingdom. John 17 speaks of the oneness that Jesus prayed over us, His church. Here Jesus says, "I pray that they will all be one, just as you and I are one—as you are in me, Father, and I am in you. And may they be in us so that the world will believe you sent me" (John 17:21 NLT). This holy oneness is only possible when we're fully abandoned in Christ, prioritizing unity in the Spirit over agreement on the issues. This doesn't mean neglecting issues of holiness but rather clinging to its purest form, which is love. See, no matter how singularly focused we may be on our worthy goals of peace, justice, and equality, they actually can't happen without an undergirding sense that we belong to each other. A unified church is a serious threat to the kingdom of darkness. Why else do you think Satan would work so hard to undermine our oneness? But if we're to remain one with God and with each other, we must refuse to allow anything to separate us, we must prefer one another over ourselves, and we must prioritize the kingdom of God above all else. Church, we've been commissioned as an outpost of heaven. We can't afford to settle for mere agreement or sameness when there's a watching world that needs to witness a unity so otherworldly that only Christ's love could explain it.

REFLECTIONS

1. The Gospel is clear: Jesus didn't come to start a new religion; He came to form a new spiritual family. As you consider your experience of church, has it looked more like a corporate blueprint that has people climbing ladders of ambition or like a family where people sit at tables together and hearts are imprinted by heavenly affection? What are the implications of each?

2. With most congregations in America having 80 to 90 percent of the work being done by 10 to 20 percent of the people, we've left little opportunity for others to grow in their gifts and callings. Consumerism then mustn't be seen as a foe to defeat but rather as a friendship we've consistently chosen over the family God has entrusted to us. The only real solution to this problem is to be intentional about having the "professionals" do less. What would this look like in the context of your church? What challenges can you foresee in relaxing perfectionistic standards of performance to give way to grace-filled opportunities for trial and error?

3. In John 13:14–35 (NIV), Jesus gives us the command to love one another—the key that lets the world know we've been sent by God. To know the love of God is to truly find Him irresistible. So in the midst of all the culture wars, what would happen if we set our differences aside and decided that the enemy of our enemy is actually our friend—worthy of our love, loyalty, and liberation? What if instead of being known for the points we make with our lips, we were known for the difference we make with our lives? What if we were known by who we're for rather than what we're against? What if we were able to love lost people more than lost people love their sin?

4. The fact is anyplace there's pain, heartache, and need, God lives there. And if God is near to such people and places, don't you think His people should be there also? What would happen if we were to model a unity so otherworldly that only Christ's love could explain it? How might the world change as a result? What can we learn from Jesus's story of the Good Samaritan?

CHAPTER 7

THE SHOUTING

The Bible records the final moments of Christ's life on earth, saying, "When He had received the drink, Jesus said, 'It is finished.' With that, He bowed His head and gave up His spirit" (John 19:30 NIV). Mark records the account this way: "With a loud cry, Jesus breathed His last" (Mark 15:37 NIV). Therefore, it's a commonly held belief by many scholars that this "loud cry" was likely to have been those very last words that John records, "It is finished." This wasn't the despairing cry of a helpless martyr or a sigh of relief from a worn-out life. As Jesus heaved upward to take His final breath, He gathered enough air to give a mighty victory shout for all the world to know and for every demonic force to flee because in that instant, He had finished the work His Father sent Him to do.

In the exact moment Caiaphas, the high priest, made his annual entrance into the holy of holies to offer the blood of the Passover lamb on the Day of Atonement, the perfect Lamb of God became the ultimate sacrifice, fully atoning for man's sin. There was now no more penalty left to be paid, no further need for the sacrificial system of Old Testament law. Christ's blood was infinitely superior to that of animals, and it would be all sufficient for all of time. A new covenant was now in effect, ushering in an era of grace. No longer would man engage in religious transactions to settle accounts with God while racking up a tab of daily debts. The implications of this sudden and dramatic shift in how we relate to God would alone be enough to secure our eternal destination in heaven, but in remarkable fashion, the plan of God would be even greater still!

Miles away from Golgotha, inside the temple at Jerusalem, an inexplicable, supernatural event occurred. While the world was shrouded in darkness from noon until three o'clock, at the precise time Jesus declared, "It is finished," the massive, fortified veil that stood before the holy of holies was suddenly torn in half from top to bottom. This veil was reportedly sixty feet high, thirty feet wide, and an estimated four inches thick. One early Jewish writing states that the veil was so heavy it took three hundred priests to move or manipulate it. While this may have been hyperbole to some extent, if even a fraction of this claim were true, it would have been humanly impossible to tear such a veil. I can only imagine the sound it would have produced as the people watched in complete amazement. Just think what must have gone through Caiaphas's mind when he saw that the way to the holy of holies had been opened and he was no longer needed to enter in on behalf of the people!

Because of the finished work of Jesus on the cross at Golgotha, we can now enter into a new way of life marked by debt-free living and unfathomable friendship with God that'll cause us to boldly join our voices with His in celebratory shouts of victory! What we are now able to enjoy is the prophetic fulfillment of Psalm 27:4 (NKJV) that says, "One thing I have desired of the Lord, that will I seek: that I may dwell in the house of the Lord all the days of my life, to behold the beauty of the Lord, and to inquire in His temple." We now have unfettered access to the powerful, continual presence of God dwelling in us as living temples of the Holy Spirit. What an incredible gift we now have as a result of that veil being torn! This divinely inspired connection with God is a vital component of a healthy Christian life. When we're deeply connected to the Father, we're adequately prepared for seasons of victory and seasons of battle. David seemingly understood this, which is why he didn't ask for

God to give him a platform of influence, a throne of power, or even a voice to lead. Instead, when David could've asked for anything, he asked God to make him a beholder of the beauty of the Lord. Do we take seriously the reality that we reflect what we revere? Do we truly believe that we'll ultimately become what we behold?

As A.W. Tozer said, "When God is exalted to the right place in our lives, a thousand problems are solved all at once." David understood that the key to having a right heart and leading others into freedom and prosperity was to gaze upon the Lord's beauty—to be attentive to whatever God wanted to show him. Similarly, Jesus said that He only did what He saw His Father doing (John 5:19 NLT) and He only said what He heard His Father saying (John 12:49 NLT). Today, I believe there are still things God gets excited about and things that grieve His heart. If we don't make it our prayer to become beholders of His beauty, we may find ourselves so busied by other activities that, like the disciples, Jesus would say to us, "You have eyes—can't you see? You have ears—can't you hear?" (Mark 8:18 NLT). What a terrifying thought—that we could miss the beauty of an unveiled God who invites us to come into His presence because we've become preoccupied with lesser things!

There's no shortage of problems in our world today, problems for which many solutions have been tried and proposed, yet these problems continue to persist. The voices of politicians, celebrities, and television pundits weigh in, diagnose, and debate, making headlines and dominating airwaves. Yet Jesus didn't waste His breath over such things. Could it be that what we've called problems are, in fact, mere symptoms? Could it be that the real problem at the root of it all is that because we've turned our attention to the noise of the world, much of the church has become deafened to the voice of God? Turning up the volume on the voices of criticism, conformity, and condemnation, many Christians no longer allow themselves enough quiet for God to get a word in edgewise. While the problem and its many symptoms can be discouraging, we can take heart in the words of Jesus when He said, "My sheep listen to my voice; I know them, and they follow me" (John 10:27 NLT). The Good Shepherd continues to speak, and if we'll listen, there's still time to correct course and follow to the place of abundance where He leads.

A basic principle of audiology we're all familiar with is that the noise around you will affect your ability to listen. So naturally, the quieter someone speaks, the closer you have to get to hear them. Recently, my youngest daughter, who was five years old at the time, was playing on her tablet upstairs (I know, stellar parenting, right? Mom was gone.) And wouldn't you know the absolute worst thing that could possibly happen occurred in that moment? Yep, you guessed it! She lost her Wi-Fi connection. (Dun-dun-dun!) So the next thing I know, I'm hearing her little voice getting louder and louder, trying to get my attention from upstairs.

Now, to teach her that hollering across the house isn't the way to get our attention, I decided I'd answer her as quietly as I could to be heard but not understood, and sure enough, she kept getting closer and closer until she could hear me clearly. Now, that's not to say that if I'd hollered back at her from the other side of the house, I couldn't make my voice be heard. Sure, I could. But what could get lost in all that shouting is that although she might be able to hear my words, she'd almost certainly miss her daddy's heart. And you know, she might even end up thinking I'm mad at her.

Here's the thing. It's easy to think that about God when we keep Him at a distance, isn't it? So although there are times when the Lord will raise His voice, I believe He typically chooses to speak in a whisper because God doesn't just want us to hear His voice; He wants us to know His heart. And what a whisper will do is cause us to lean in and draw close to Him. Ultimately, if you get close enough to someone, you'll be able to hear them whisper over even the noisiest surroundings. My concern is that when we're content to simply relay God's message to people, they won't lean in close enough to hear His whisper for themselves.

For the apostles, it would have been unthinkable that a person would call themselves a Christian (a follower of Christ) yet not listen to His voice or obey its leading. However, that's the regretful position we find ourselves in within the church today. Having settled for forms of godliness that have no power (2 Timothy 3:5 NIV), many Sunday-morning gatherings place little emphasis on *beholding* for fear that it may cause some to miss out on a sense of *belonging*. In reality, this tradeoff has only stood to reduce the potential of the people from becoming like God to becoming like His shiniest performers the viewing audience can behold on stage or streaming on their smart device at home. And if becoming like them is the goal, then we're in big trouble!

These gifted and often attractive few fill every minute of a one-hour service, designed to be appealing to seekers and unbelievers before quickly turning the auditorium over for the next service that's typically a near exact replica of the first. Is this the fellowship of the brethren we're strongly warned not to forsake, or were we meant to have an encounter that leads us to behold God's beauty? Are we called to merely be appealing to men, or are we called to appeal to heaven on behalf of earth? Are we supposed to entertain the masses or sing to an audience of one, entertaining the very presence of God that changes us?

In this hour, as the culture shouts loudly, preaching its own sermons and discipling a generation into a lifestyle of compromise and confusion, may the church of Jesus Christ hear the shout of heaven once again and join our voices with God's in declaring that a way has been made for humanity to press into His presence. People won't enter into the holy of holies simply because we press in with our opinions or our politics but because we press into the power of a living Gospel that continues to be accompanied by miracles, signs, and wonders (Mark 16:17–18 NLT). Our soft preaching will not be enough to till the soil of hard hearts, and our motivational messages will not provide the power needed to deliver them from demonic strongholds.

As Pastor Kevin Wallace said, "This model on which we built church for the last twenty years of seeker-only influence where it's about how quickly we get them in, how quickly we get their money, how quickly we get them out and how quickly we can produce another service that doesn't have any interruptions and goes in our forty-two-minute schedule—that thing has crested and crashed. Because what we found in the last twenty years is you cannot knock the rebellion out of the rebellious with a cute little service on Sunday." We must make room for the unscripted moments of the Spirit in our gatherings. We must make room for silence if we want God to speak. And we must make room for corporate times of prayer if we're going to enter into the holy of holies and behold His beauty. Anything else, and we may as well just put the curtain back in place, hire Caiaphas back as high priest, and resume our animal sacrifices. See, intimate relationship with God will always be an enigma for people who prefer having a mediator over having a personal encounter.

While the voice of man can *communicate* with his words, only God can *create* with each word that He breathes into existence—speaking planets into orbit and peace into storms. There are things God wants to deposit into our lives in a span of minutes that man couldn't create in many years. In fact, we must be on guard against any revelation that doesn't bring us into greater encounter or we run the risk of it only training us to be more religious. The truth is, once you've beheld the beauty and glory of God for yourself, it'll mark you to the point that you'd never want to trade it for the most brilliant of orators or the most impressive of shows. This is the moment when people stop caring about who's preaching or what songs are going to be sung. To get lost in His presence is where true and lasting value can be found. In response to the scriptural assurance that Jesus opened a new and life-giving way through the curtain, so we can now boldly enter heaven's most holy place (Hebrews 10:19–20 NLT), may we offer these types of encounters in our gatherings. May people leave our meetings more than entertained, but may they leave *awed* by Him, stirred in their spirits to pursue His presence all the more.

REFLECTIONS

1. David didn't ask for God to give him a platform of influence, a throne of power, or even a voice to lead. Instead, when David could've asked for anything, he asked God to make him a beholder of the beauty of the Lord (Psalm 27:4 NKJV). Do you take seriously the reality that you reflect what you revere? Do you truly believe that you'll ultimately become what you behold? How is it that people who know Jesus can still miss the beauty of an unveiled God who invites us to come into His presence? How is it that we can allow ourselves to get preoccupied with lesser things?

2. What do you think about the notion that much of what we've called problems are, in fact, symptoms and that the real problem at the root of it all is that much of the church has become deafened to the voice of God because we've turned our attention to the shouts of the world? In what ways have you recognized the voices of criticism, conformity, and condemnation becoming louder than the whisper of heaven that speaks calm in the midst of the storm?

3. Many Sunday-morning gatherings place little emphasis on beholding God's beauty for fear that it may cause some to miss out on a sense of belonging. Do you see these two concepts as being at odds with each other? How do you think prioritizing belonging over beholding has reduced the potential of people to become like God? If you aren't beholding God in the gathering, and are instead beholding the performance of whoever's standing on the stage, do you suppose there's a risk of us lowering the bar from becoming like God to just becoming like one of His

shiniest performers in the spotlight? What standard do you use to measure your life?

4. Practically speaking, how does appealing to men differ from appealing to heaven on behalf of earth? How does entertaining the masses differ from singing to an audience of one, entertaining the very presence of God that changes us? How do you think a seeker-only influence emphasizes the wrong things and can limit people who are far from Jesus from actually encountering Him?

CHAPTER 8

THE SHAKING

Immediately after the victory shout of Jesus, we read in Matthew 27 that "The earth shook, rocks split apart, and tombs opened. The bodies of many godly men and women who had died were raised from the dead. They left the cemetery after Jesus' resurrection, went into the holy city of Jerusalem, and appeared to many people" (Matthew 27:51–53 NLT). What becomes immediately apparent here is that although Israel rejected Jesus and the Roman authorities crucified Him, creation *always* recognized Him! Jesus underscored this truth when He replied to the Pharisees urging Him to silence His disciples for shouting and singing praises to God for the great miracles they'd seen. He said, "I tell you, if these were silent, the very stones would cry out" (Luke 19:40 ESV). As I sought the mind of Christ in this aspect of what happened at Golgotha, these words burned in my heart—"Holy fear is the key to unlocking the fullness of resurrection life."

As I contemplated these words, my mind was instantly taken back to the moment I first encountered the Lord. I was seventeen years old, mischievous, and dead set on destroying my life. Hooked on drugs and alcohol, I didn't know how to enjoy myself when sober, except to take frequent hits from the intoxicating chemical of adrenaline. Breaking into buildings, compulsively stealing, vandalizing, and thrill seeking had become my way of life, which I resorted to as a way to escape intense feelings of depression and thoughts of suicide. I'd recently teamed up with the biggest drug dealer in my high school, and I was in possession of several dozen pounds of marijuana that I planned to move over the course of the next several weeks. This was the start of what I had foolishly planned to turn into a lucrative career, and nothing and no one was going to stop me.

Growing up in Madison, Wisconsin, I'd never met a single Christian kid in school. No one told me about Jesus, invited me to church, or even attended a youth group to my knowledge. But there was a slightly older guy at the movie theater I worked at who talked a lot about God. He began asking me questions that caused me to examine what I believed, and I began reading books on the different religions of the world. Having seen my share of hypocritical churchgoers in my young life, I'd already dismissed the notion of Christianity as mere sentimentalism and refused to explore it. Instead, I began a thorough investigation into Judaism, Islam, Hinduism, Buddhism, and New Age, only to discover none of those religions offered anything of appeal to me either. Hopeless, confused, and exhausted, I felt like just giving up on life.

I was fresh off throwing a massive party in the basement of my house and still surrounded by drug paraphernalia and empty liquor bottles in my bedroom when I decided I'd toss up one final Hail Mary on pursuing greater meaning in life. I had no Bible, I'd attended no church, and I hadn't listened to any televangelists. I remember I just knelt at my bedside, closed my eyes, and prayed what was the first honest, from the heart prayer I'd ever prayed in my whole life. All my prayer consisted of were these simple words: "God, I don't know who you are. I don't know if you're a he, a she, or an it, but if you'll just tell me your name, I promise I'll follow you all the days of my life." And that's when it happened—the instant my life would be changed forever. All alone in my room, I heard an audible voice from heaven. Somehow, it was both the loudest and softest voice I'd ever heard all at once. It was simultaneously the scariest and yet the most peaceful moment I'd ever experienced. And all I heard spoken was just one word—"Jesus."

My heart was gripped with holy fear as I literally began searching all around me, trying to figure out where that voice could have possibly come from. I searched throughout the entire house, looking for an answer that would explain what had just happened to me, but there was no one. And suddenly, I felt different—lighter, happier, and free. In that brief encounter, with just one word spoken by God to a juvenile delinquent steeped in sin, I was made brand-new from the inside out. I was instantly freed from my addiction to drugs and alcohol. The desire to lie, cheat, and steal was eradicated from my heart. Thoughts of worthlessness and suicide were replaced with the revelation that I was seen, known, and loved by my Creator. This D and F student facing truancy charges became an A and B student who consistently attended class, all because Jesus had given me a reason to live, a reason to try to please Him with my life.

No one had to tell me to repent or to change. Just as the earthquake opened those tombs and made dead men live in response to Christ's shout of victory from the cross, His shout to me that day produced a mighty shaking that brought me out of my grave also, and the natural response of my heart was to be gripped with a holy fear that wouldn't let me forget the vows I had made to the Lord—that I would live for Him all the days of my life. As scripture teaches, "Fear of the Lord is the foundation of wisdom" (Proverbs 9:10 NLT) and "All who fear the Lord will hate evil" (Proverbs 8:13 NLT). The answer to the problems of sin and compromise plaguing the church today is to return to the place of holy fear, to once again tremble in His presence and commit to keep the vows we've made to the Lord—to realize that one of the greatest enemies to God's will for our lives is *our* will for our lives. And since we are but dead men walking, may we never forget that our will for our lives leads only back to the tomb from which we came—back to the place of emptiness and hopelessness Jesus delivered us from.

Leonard Ravenhill once said, "A man with an experience of God is never at the mercy of a man with an argument, for an experience of God that costs something is worth something, and does something." Several months after I surrendered my life to Jesus, I had a police officer show up at my front door. Upon answering it, he began to question me about some stolen merchandise that had turned up at a local pawn shop. It seemed one of my friends who I'd traded some items to had been arrested and gave my name to the authorities. In that moment, I was reminded of the vows I made to God as a result of my experience with Him. I could've easily lied to the officer and been spared the consequences, but in doing so, I knew I'd be turning my back on the Lord. Instead, I owned up to everything I had done, and I repaid my debts to society. After completing the Scared Straight program, performing a hundred hours of community service, and paying $1,000 in restitution, I had no regrets. The holy fear in my heart wasn't me being afraid of God; it was me being afraid of being *away from* Him. The freedom and joy I had found in Jesus were worth any price I had to pay to stay free from my old tomb!

In the midst of the shaking that's going on in the world, and especially in the church today, I believe God is appealing to His people to be holy as He is holy (1 Peter 1:16 NLT). A renewed call to holiness needs to be issued from pulpits and on podcasts, in places of worship, and on radio airwaves. No more compromise! No more playing religious games! It's time for us to get back to the place of working out our salvation with fear and trembling—to return to our first love. We need a fresh experience of God that costs something, is worth something, and does something. The trouble with holiness and the church over the years is that purity has been portrayed as piety and packaged as legalism. But the reality is that the pollution of carnality will continue to flood the hearts of those in the pews if there's no power coming from our pulpits, and there can be no power without a purity that results from the potency of God's presence. We need to get back to the place of Pentecost that like the early church, it might be said of us that after we prayed, the place where we were meeting was shaken, that we were all filled with the Holy Spirit and spoke the word of God boldly (Acts 4:31 NLT). This is still God's design—the church prays, God shakes the church, and the church shakes the world. Those with eyes that see and ears that hear can perceive heaven's urgent appeal to pray fervently and burn with holy fire, that our lives wouldn't be marked by compromise but by consecration, purity, and passion.

Many have become bored in their walk with God, which is why they've disengaged from the battle, and like King David on the rooftop, they've been in a place they have no business being, beholding lesser lovers that only serve to make them impotent for the kingdom (2 Samuel 11 NLT). But the truth is if you find yourself bored in your walk with God, you're not actually walking with Him at all. The boredom you're experiencing is the number one by-product of dead religion. When David shifted the lens of his worship and focused it on Bathsheba, he made much of her and little of the Lord. It's no wonder he suffered great personal loss, destruction in his family, and defeat to the nation he was supposed to be leading in freedom and victory. We run the same risk, but if we take the lens of our worship and focus it back on the throne of God and the precious Lamb who sits upon it, when lesser things vie for our attention, we won't be distracted.

Don't be too quick to dismiss these words as legalism. Those who aren't married to the Bridegroom will often criticize those who are because loyalty will always look like legalism to the one who isn't in love. We would be wise to heed the words of Hebrews 12 that say, "Be careful that you do not refuse to listen to the One who is speaking. For if the people of Israel did not escape when they refused to listen to Moses, the earthly messenger, we will certainly not escape if we reject the One who speaks to us from heaven! When God spoke from Mount Sinai His voice shook the earth, but now He makes another promise: 'Once again I will shake not only the earth but the heavens also.' This means that all of creation will be shaken and removed, so that only unshakable things will remain. Since we are receiving a Kingdom that is unshakable, let us be thankful and please God by worshiping Him with holy fear and awe. For our God is a devouring fire" (Hebrews 12:25–29 NLT). Don't confuse shaking with breaking. One purifies where the other destroys. What may look like pain is often the very process God uses to make His people potent.

May we not be casual about our prayer lives or flippant about revival. May we not live as though we have the luxury of time on our side, hitting the snooze button on the alarm of heaven intended to awaken us from our slumber in this very hour. The shaking that's been happening and will continue to happen should serve as a sign to us that it's time to stop resisting the holy fear and awe necessary to encounter the all-consuming fire of God. May we place greater emphasis on character and integrity than we do on gifts and anointing. May we not merely pay lip service to the Holy Spirit in our songs and in our preaching, but may our lives be marked by a godly sorrow that leads to true repentance for all the times we've structured Him out of our services—for all the ways we've made our gatherings about us instead of Him, placing our agenda ahead of His. May there be fire from our pulpits once more that we wouldn't render a generation weak and helpless by nice preaching and feel-good messages made to tickle ears.

At the end of the day, what we should fear far above failing at the things that matter to us is succeeding at the things that don't really matter in light of eternity. Jesus made this distinction crystal clear to the religious leaders of His day when He said, "What sorrow awaits you teachers of religious law and you Pharisees. Hypocrites! For you are like whitewashed tombs—beautiful on the outside but filled on the inside with dead people's bones and all sorts of impurity. Outwardly you look like righteous people, but inwardly your hearts are filled with hypocrisy and lawlessness" (Matthew 23:27–28 NLT). The danger Jesus warns them about is emphasizing physical appearances over spiritual realities—external performance over internal purity. When the shaking comes to a tomb like that, sadly nothing will emerge from it but the stench of death and duplicity, but a healthy fear of God that keeps us close to Him is what will ignite fresh zeal in our hearts and cause us to become unshakeable.

God's looking for an intimate relationship with those who fear Him (Psalm 25:14 NLT), and as Paul writes to the church at Philippi, it's in those who work out their own salvation with fear and trembling that God works to will and to act in order to fulfill His good purpose—that which pleases Him (Philippians 2:12 NIV). As we read further in this passage, we're given a clue to what it means to fulfill God's good purpose in our lives. In verse 15, Paul tells the Philippians to shine like bright lights in this world—a strikingly similar statement to the words of Jesus in the Sermon on the Mount, in which He tells the disciples, "You are the light of the world—like a city on a hilltop that cannot be hidden" (Matthew 5:14 NLT). In order for us to fully appreciate the impact of Jesus's words here, we must understand that in God's kingdom, light represents bringing order out of chaos.

Consider the creation account in Genesis where God said, "Let there be light" (Genesis 1:3 NLT) and order emerged from the chaos of darkness. As the church, each of us are meant to minister to the broken and hurting. When we do so, we shine as radiant light and order is brought to the chaos of people's lives. This is what Jesus means in Luke 11:36 (NLT) when He said His followers would be full of light; our whole lives shining brightly for God's glory. The fullness of resurrection life is unlocked by the shaking that comes when we fear the Lord. We obey Him in reverent awe, radiating the light of Christ and releasing faith for God to do the miraculous among the tombs of a lost and dying world. May we once again be shaken so all that remains would be the unshakeable kingdom permeating our lives and churches to shine brighter than ever before!

REFLECTIONS

1. What's been your experience with the subject of holiness in the church? What problems have arisen when it's been portrayed as piety or packaged as legalism? How does your view of purity shift when you hear that it's actually the power that results from the potency of God's presence?

2. At the victory shout of Jesus in Matthew 27 (NLT), the shaking that occurred opened tombs, and the bodies of many godly men and women who'd died were raised to life. In contrast, Jesus called the religious leaders of his day "whitewashed tombs" because outwardly they looked righteous, but inwardly their hearts were filled with hypocrisy and sin. In other words, there were literal dead people who carried more life in their bones than the Pharisees did. What's the difference between biblical holiness and religious rule keeping?

3. In 2 Timothy 3:5 (NIV), we're warned about people who have a form (appearance) of godliness but deny the power that could actually make them holy, and we're warned strongly to stay away from such people. What's the danger of disregarding this warning? How can a healthy fear of God keep us close to Him?

4. What does Hebrews 12:28 (NLT) mean when it says that we "please God by worshiping Him with holy fear and awe"? Practically speaking, what does that look like in a believer's life?

5. Since light in God's Word represents bringing order out of chaos, we understand that when we shine radiantly as the lights Christ intended, order can be brought to the chaos of people's

lives. As we examine the darkness of our world today and the chaos all around, what does it say about the church as a whole when it comes to shining our light? How do you think we're doing? What needs to change if we're going to be the difference God designed us to be?

6. Read Acts 2:1–4 and Acts 16:16–34. When was the last time you or your church held a prayer meeting? In what ways, if any, did it resemble the prayer meetings of Acts? What got shaken?

CHAPTER 9

THE FOUNTAINHEAD

A natural spring that's the principal source of a stream is known as a fountainhead. The water that originates from a fountainhead is said to be exceptionally pure, healthy to the body, and have a sweet taste to it. It makes perfect sense then that Jesus would be referred to as the Fountainhead. The Gospel of John makes frequent reference to Jesus as our source of life with well-known passages that say things like "For God so loved the world that He gave His one and only Son, that whoever believes in Him shall not perish but have *eternal life*" (John 3:16 NIV). In another familiar verse of John's Gospel, Jesus tells us, "The thief comes only to steal and kill and destroy; I have come that they may have *life*, and have it to the *full*" (John 10:10 NIV). These two verses point toward the reason that John's Gospel is often referred to as the Gospel of life—because of its emphasis on Jesus as our source. So when we consider the details in John's account of Christ's crucifixion, we need to keep that emphasis in mind.

At Golgotha, we see that the "soldiers came and broke the legs of the two men crucified with Jesus. But when they came to Jesus, they saw that He was already dead, so they didn't break His legs. One of the soldiers, however, pierced His side with a spear, and immediately blood and water flowed out" (John 19:32–34 NLT). Jesus is said to have experienced something called hypovolemic shock, which produced a rapid heartbeat and caused fluid to gather in the sack around His heart and lungs. This explains why, after Jesus died and a Roman soldier thrust a spear through Jesus's side, piercing both the lungs and the heart, blood and water poured out from His side. However, John's Gospel makes clear that these things were more than mere medical symptomology.

Like everything recorded in scripture about Christ's virgin birth, sinless life, miraculous ministry, sacrificial death, and glorious resurrection, these things represented profound spiritual realities. In this case, what's depicted for us is that the death of Jesus opened two fountains to meet all our needs—the blood formed a fountain for the washing away of sin (Zechariah 13:1 NLT), and the water became the fountain of divine life (Psalm 36:9 NLT; Revelation 21:6 NLT). Whoever believes in Jesus drinks from these fountains, and the Bible promises streams of living water will flow from within them (John 7:37–38 NLT). In other words, He makes every believer into a fountainhead because of the Holy Spirit's power at work in us! We have been created anew to reproduce redemption and divine life as we minister the Gospel message of Christ's shed blood by the Spirit of God that dwells within us—that living water marked by exceptionally purity, providing health to the body and a sweetness that allows people to taste and see that the Lord is good (Psalm 34:8 NLT).

What a concept—that the Lord of Creation would choose us as His vessels to work through! I mean, really take a minute to think about that. If a hole was poked in you right now, what would pour out of your life? What would the symptomology of your spiritual condition be? It's one thing to *drink from* the Fountainhead. It's something entirely different to *become* a fountainhead. I don't know about you, but there are certainly moments in my day to day when I'm not exactly producing the kind of redemption and divine life that others should have any confidence in drinking from. And there are times when my natural thinking takes over and I've convinced myself it's not even possible. Yet I'm reminded that God is looking for people through whom He can do the impossible. And isn't it a shame that our plans often include only the things that we can do by ourselves?

Now, before you retreat to the place of false humility—you know the one where you say, "I'm just a sinner saved by grace," and you minimize your role in the kingdom—I'd like to remind you that it was Jesus who boldly declared of you, "I tell you the truth, *anyone* who believes in me will do the same works I have done, and *even greater* works, because I am going to be with the Father" (John 14:12 NLT). Please don't get me wrong; I'm not saying you should equate yourself with Jesus or claim to be anyone special. No, I'm saying that Jesus equated you with Himself and claimed you can be someone special. So I hope you don't mind me getting all up in your business for a second, but I've just got to ask you—who do you think you are to contradict the Master? What makes you so sure that your living small is a sign of your humility and not your pride that would prefer to play it safe so as not to fail and make a fool of yourself?

Doing the will of the Father isn't merely attending a weekly church service, listening to a good Bible teacher, or memorizing a few Bible verses; it's going and doing what scripture commands, especially as it pertains to laboring in the harvest fields. As we obey, the doorway is opened to His promises, and we grow an appetite for the impossible. Those who've drank from the Fountainhead know firsthand the power of its redemption and life-giving supply. Our spiritual taste buds have been divinely reordered in such a way that what we now thirst for is to see the impossibilities around us bow at the name of Jesus. Our deep desire for others to experience this redemption and abundance of life supersedes our pride and fear, causing us to give God our "yes" to being vessels He can flow His power through—people who understand that it's supposed to look impossible because that's how God gets the glory.

It doesn't make sense that a pure and holy God would work through imperfect people like you and me, but at its core, that's what faith is—it's trusting what we cannot see more than what we can see. It's going without knowing, resting in the assurance that with every command God gives always comes the power to be effective in what He's calling us to do. It's living in such a way that, unless God intervenes, what you're attempting to do is sure to fail. It's refusing to settle for the best you can do in a given situation and instead striving for the best God can do through you. See, it's only when you recognize the gap between your capabilities and God's calling that you're able to see your need for God's supernatural empowerment.

People are filled with all kinds of things these days—pride, hatred, jealousy, greed, and the list goes on. On our own, we can only be filled with ourselves, living for ourselves and limited by our fallen nature. For streams of living water to burst forth out of us, we must heed the command of scripture to be filled with the Holy Spirit (Ephesians 5:18 NLT). It's then that you're filled with the kind of wisdom that comes from above (James 3:17 NLT). It's then that you're filled with joy unspeakable and full of glory (1 Peter 1:8 KJV). And it's then that you're filled with power to be a bold witness for Christ (Acts 1:8 NLT). See, whatever you're full of is what will inevitably spill over. It's not about being worthy. It's not about becoming weird. It's about recognizing your own weakness and surrendering to God's ways to do what you could never do on your own.

In chapter 13 of the book of Acts, we see that "the disciples were continually filled [throughout their hearts and souls] with joy and with the Holy Spirit" (Acts 13:52 AMP). Just like them, there's an assignment of heaven on your life, and you won't be able to fulfill it if you're filled up on the wrong stuff. Regardless of denomination, geography, or vocation, every Christian believer needs to be routinely filled to overflowing with the Spirit of God. It's how time and again revival has swept over our churches and communities. It's how movements were ignited that resulted in millions of souls saved. It's how the church was birthed on the day of Pentecost over two thousand years ago, and the Spirit-filled life is still the only hope for us to reach a lost and dying world today. To personalize this, let me say it this way—God's solution to a sin-filled world is you, full of the Spirit. By His Spirit, you'll change atmospheres; atmospheres won't change you. So drink deeply of the refreshing fountain of the Holy Spirit who fills you up to send hell running!

Toward the end of John's Gospel, Jesus is headed to the cross. He knows He's going to be leaving this world soon, so He prepares His disciples by introducing them to the most important person on His mind—the Holy Spirit. Listen to His words to them in the midst of their grieving: "I am telling you the truth: it is better for you that I go away, because if I do not go, the Helper will not come to you. But if I do go away, then I will send him to you" (John 16:7 GNT). Now, when Jesus says, "I am telling you the truth," He's basically saying, "You may find this hard to believe, but what I'm about to tell you is a really big deal!" Jesus is telling His followers here that it's actually *better* for them to have the Holy Spirit with them than to have Jesus with them. And it was true not only for His followers back then but for us today also. It's better for you and I to have the invisible Holy Spirit than to have a physical Jesus with us. See, when Jesus was here on the earth, He could be beside one person at one time, doing one thing. But now, the Spirit of God is on the inside of every believer and can help everyone everywhere. Simply put, God's Word says that the Holy Spirit *inside* you is better than Jesus *beside* you.

So no matter where you go and no matter what you face, He's with you! You're never alone, outmatched, overpowered, or outnumbered. With the Holy Spirit, you're always enough, always victorious, always a majority in any situation you encounter. God didn't put His Holy Spirit in you just so you could safely arrive at your destination and slide into the pearly gates of heaven one day. You're filled with His presence to make you a force to be reckoned with in this world. You're called to win battles in the heavenly realms, to tear down enemy strongholds and set captives free by the power of God. You have the ability to lift the atmosphere of every room you walk into because you're a living container of resurrection power (Romans 8:11 NIV). This was the normative experience for every New Testament believer. So why would you settle for a drop when Jesus declares there's a fountain? Why settle for a morsel when He says there's a feast?

We owe it to our children and their children to receive all that God has because here's what I know—whatever isn't *transformed* in one generation will inevitably get *transferred* to the next. Let's determine that the bondage and oppression plaguing our nation today would be broken in Jesus's name! May we be empowered by the Spirit to live supernaturally. When someone comes to you for advice or for prayer and you honestly just don't have the words, the Holy Spirit will give you the words to say. He'll use you to bring comfort, counsel, compassion, and sometimes even loving correction when it's needed in somebody's life. He'll give you things to say that'll often leave that person asking you, "How could you have possibly known that?" because the Holy Spirit will fill your mouth with words of knowledge and words of wisdom that'll speak directly to the issues in a person's heart (1 Corinthians 12:4–11 NLT). He'll use you to prophetically strengthen, comfort, and encourage the people around you, all for God's glory (1 Corinthians 14:3 NLT). In doing so, heaven invades earth, and the kingdom of God advances.

The living water that fills you is what empowers you to accomplish the Holy Spirit's mission in the world—to produce refreshing streams through you that comfort the hurting and strengthen the weary, nourishing every thirsty soul and pointing them to the Lord Jesus. The Holy Spirit isn't just a Sunday morning at church kind of God. No, He's a Monday morning kind of God. He's a Thursday afternoon kind of God, and He's a take Him with you to work kind of God. He is the Parakletos—our Helper, Comforter, and Intercessor (John 14:16–17 NLT). He brings conviction of sin to draw hearts closer to the Father. He brings the teachings of Jesus to our remembrance to help us live for God. Christ promised and purchased the Holy Spirit's presence in your life for you to have an intimate relationship with Him, for you to use Him in your daily life, and for you to demonstrate to a watching world just how relevant the Spirit of God is.

Regardless of how long you've walked with the Lord or your level of spiritual maturity in Him, I can tell you with great confidence that there's still more because in Him is a limitless supply, a never-ending reservoir of the person, presence, and power of the Holy Spirit. If you haven't received from the Holy Spirit what the scriptures describe in Acts 2 (NLT), I'd like to encourage you to sincerely pray this simple two-part prayer: (1) God, if there's anything in me that's resistant to what You have for me, I surrender that right now; and (2) God, if there's anything You have for me that I'm not yet experiencing, I want it all. Come, Holy Spirit. Fill me afresh until I overflow. May streams of living water burst forth out of me, bringing redemption and divine life to the people around me."

As you seek a fresh infilling of God's Spirit, be encouraged by Jesus's teaching about prayer when He told His disciples this story: "Suppose you went to a friend's house at midnight, wanting to borrow three loaves of bread. You say to him, 'A friend of mine has just arrived for a visit, and I have nothing for him to eat.' And suppose he calls out from his bedroom, 'Don't bother me. The door is locked for the night, and my family and I are all in bed. I can't help you.' But I tell you this—though he won't do it for friendship's sake, if you keep knocking long enough, he will get up and give you whatever you need because of your shameless persistence. And so I tell you, keep on asking, and you will receive what you ask for. Keep on seeking, and you will find. Keep on knocking, and the door will be opened to you. For everyone who asks, receives. Everyone who seeks, finds. And to everyone who knocks, the door will be opened. You fathers—if your children ask for a fish, do you give them a snake instead? Or if they ask for an egg, do you give them a scorpion? Of course not! So if you sinful people know how to give good gifts to your children, how much more will your heavenly Father give the Holy Spirit to those who ask Him" (Luke 11:5–13 NLT). I dare you to be so bold, so persistent, and so faith filled as to approach God like this. When you do, I can assure you that you'll come to discover that God wants to fill you with His Holy Spirit even more than you want to be filled!

One of the names of God mentioned in scripture is El Shaddai, the All Sufficient One, the God of More Than Enough. The Father first revealed Himself as El Shaddai to Abram at ninety-nine years old and made covenant with him, guaranteeing Abram countless descendants. Jesus demonstrated the same nature, taking five loaves and two fish and multiplying them to feed the five thousand with twelve baskets left over. Everything God does is over the top, infinitely more than we might ask or think (Ephesians 3:20 NLT). He can never be not enough because He doesn't lack. He can never be just enough because the very essence of God takes up all the space. So anything God chooses to inhabit must expand to greater capacity. And make no mistake, when Jesus (who is the Baptizer) baptizes us with the Holy Spirit and fire (Matthew 3:11 NLT), we encounter El Shaddai in a very real sense. The God of More Than Enough will overflow when you allow Him to fill you because that's just what He does. He will expand you to greater capacity, enlarging the potential of your faith, your love, and your gifts for His glory. The Fountainhead will pour superabundance of life in you, causing you to brim in the graces of God until His goodness runs over, refreshing and reviving those He's placed in your path. Ask and you will receive. Seek and you will find. Knock and the door will be opened to you. "This gift is to you, to your children and to those far away—all who have been called by the Lord our God" (Acts 2:39 NLT). What are you waiting for? Go claim your rightful inheritance in Jesus!

As God fills us with His Spirit, He's doing more than just revealing truth to us. He's actually depositing the Spirit of revelation in us so we can partner with Him in revealing truth to our generation. As He did at the wedding feast in John 2 (NLT), the Lord is once again pouring into these vessels a new wine that isn't the product of man's efforts but is a supernatural outpouring that far exceeds the quality of what we had before. We, the church, cannot afford to cling to familiar forms associated with human effort, or we'll be left with only empty vessels, and the people will be left with nothing to drink. I've heard it said that there are three ways to live your life: waste your life, spend your life, or invest your life. But I'm going to offer a fourth—pour out your life as a drink offering to the Lord, allowing what God has poured into you to spill over so that He can fill you afresh. I think Tauren Wells put it best when he said that "The world screams, 'Make much of yourself,' while the Gospel whispers, 'Give yourself away.'" After all, it's pretty hard to argue that a hold nothing back approach in this life will leave us with any regrets in the next.

REFLECTIONS

1. When you think about the spiritual reality of being a fountainhead, created anew to reproduce redemption and divine life as streams of living water flow through you, does this excite you or intimidate you? What do you think your response says about the symptomology of your spiritual condition? In other words, if a hole was poked in you, what would pour out of your life?

2. Considering that the God of the impossible lives in you and desires to do the impossible through you, how do your plans make room for those things that you can't do by yourself and in your own power? If you would say you don't make room for the impossible, can you really say that you're making room for God? Can you truly say that you're keeping in step with the Spirit?

3. Doing the will of God requires that we obey what scripture commands. It means defining ourselves not by our own feelings or limitations but by what Jesus says about us, and He says we'll do even greater works than He did. Does that seem impossible to you? Well, it's supposed to because that's how God gets the glory. Humility isn't making yourself small; it's yielding your will to God's. As you examine your life, do you have the tendency to live small and call it humility? Do you think there's an element of pride there that would prefer to play it safe so as not to fail and make a fool of yourself? How do you move past the pride and fear that's held you back to be one who knows God and carries out great exploits for His namesake?

4. Have you ever taken the time to evaluate the gap between your capabilities and God's calling on your life? Does this cause you to recognize your need for God's supernatural empowerment?

5. The Spirit-filled life is our only hope to reach a lost and dying world. This is why Jesus tells His followers that it's actually better for them to have the Holy Spirit *inside* them than it is to have Jesus *beside* them. How does that statement strike you? Have you been filled with the living water of God's Spirit? Why settle for a drop when Jesus declares there's a fountain?

CHAPTER 10

THE STARES

Matthew's Gospel records that wise men from the east once stared into the cosmos to be led to the newborn king of the Jews who'd come to save humankind (Matthew 2:9 NLT). Mark's Gospel records that Jesus taught His disciples that one day humankind will stare up at the clouds to see the Son of Man returning with great power and glory (Mark 13:26 NLT). And Romans tells us that every person who's ever lived has stared into God's creation and seen the reflection of His invisible qualities—His eternal power and divine nature—so men are without excuse for not knowing God (Romans 1:20 NLT). In John's Gospel, we read that the things that transpired at Golgotha during Jesus's crucifixion were to fulfill Old Testament prophecy (John 19:36–37 NLT). Zechariah 12:10 (NLT) and Psalm 22:17 (NLT) are two such prophetic examples, which speak of Christ's enemies who would stare upon the one they had pierced and gloat. They were able to see the very one who is truth, yet they were unable to perceive the truth that He embodied before their very eyes.

When my wife, Megan, accepted a position as the executive director of a local nonprofit agency several years back, she began a massive renovation of the facilities that would enable them to better serve the people they were ministering to. As she shared her plans with me and the progress they were making along the way, one tiny little item stands out in my mind. In the entryway, between two glass doors, stood an artificial fichus tree that apparently had been there in that spot for many years, and it took up enough space that a person would have to duck and dodge as they entered the building so it didn't hit them in the face. Naturally, Megan identified the fichus tree as something they'd need to remove to create a more welcoming and accessible space for their clients. However, when she brought it up to some of the folks who'd been there for many years, they had absolutely no idea what she was talking about! It seems they'd stared at that fichus tree for so long and had become so accustomed to the ducking and dodging that it simply blended in with the scenery and escaped their consciousness.

Anyone who's ever come in to pastor a church or lead an organization can probably relate to this concept, as there are many aspects of church life and organizational culture that can easily become imperceptible to people over time. This is one reason why consultants are such a utilized resource—because it often takes an outsider to point out our blind spots. Jesus addresses the church of Laodicea in Revelation 3, and He points something out that should've been obvious to them, but they were unable to see. He says, "I advise you to buy gold from me—gold that has been purified by fire. Then you will be rich. Also buy white garments from me so you will not be shamed by your nakedness, and ointment for your eyes so you will be able to see" (Revelation 3:18 NLT). The church of Laodicea saw themselves as rich, having everything they wanted. Yet Jesus uses words like wretched, miserable, poor, blind, and naked to describe them. Wow, it's amazing how far off their assessment of themselves was! What Jesus was telling them was that though they had the riches of heaven available to them, their indifference and complacency had blinded them to what was right before their eyes.

There were seven churches Jesus addressed in the book of Revelation; however, Laodicea is the only one who receives no praise from Him, only rebuke. Their contentment with worldly wealth had rotted their worship and rendered them worthless in service to the kingdom of God. They were lukewarm, lazy lovers of self who weren't concerned for the lost. Their salt had lost its saltiness (Matthew 5:13 NIV), and they'd blown their witness by becoming like the world while bearing the name of Christ. This was blasphemous, and Jesus warns them that He's about to spit them out of His mouth because it was disgusting to Him that they called themselves a church.

See, hot and cold water both have uses that benefit people, either as a therapeutic agent of healing or as a thirst-quenching agent of refreshing. However, lukewarm water is completely useless. We were meant to serve the people Christ came to serve—to embody His heart and embrace our redemptive role in His mission. Those lost in the self-reliant rat race of this world won't come to know the healing and refreshing their souls so desperately need if we're just like the world, prioritizing self and caring only for our own. The warning for us here is that there's a danger in staring too long at the wrong things. When we live for ourselves, we've got a staring problem. Fixated on our own wants and ignoring the needs of the people around us, we're useless, and we've lost our purpose. Can I submit to you that what exists in your blind spots may be the very things God is trying to bring into focus today, so that like the church of Laodicea, you won't be spit from Jesus's mouth?

As Charles Spurgeon once said, "Selfishness cannot be trusted with power in prayer. Unloving spirits cannot be trusted with great, broad, unlimited promises. If God is to hear us, we must love God and each other. For when we love God, we shall not pray for anything that would not honor God and shall not wish to see anything happen that would not also bless our brethren. You must get rid of selfishness before God can trust you with the keys of heaven, but when self is dead, then He will enable you to unlock His treasuries."

Scripture tells us that "the eyes of the Lord search the whole earth in order to strengthen those whose hearts are fully committed to Him" (2 Chronicles 16:9 NLT). The beautiful truth revealed here is that when the focus of our heart is fixed on God, it positions us to receive what we need from Him. When we operate in this way, we step into the realm of faith, which is the currency of the kingdom needed to free us from the trap of self-reliance. If your heart's feeling the pull of Holy Spirit conviction, why not allow truth revealed to push you toward truth experienced that you would live your life for those Christ gave His life for? All hope wasn't lost for those in Laodicea. Toward the end of the chapter, Jesus extends this incredible invitation for them to stare into His eyes, listen to His voice, and eat from His table. He says, "Look! I stand at the door and knock. If you hear my voice and open the door, I will come in, and we will share a meal together as friends" (Revelation 3:20 NLT). I assure you that when you look, listen, and eat, you'll find that your vision, hearing, and taste buds will begin to change to be more like His!

There's a whole lot of pain and brokenness all around us every day. It's a wonder people still watch the nightly news when it's never good. Yet people do. Why? Well, one of the paradoxical truths about humanity is that we often only glance at what's beautiful, but we gaze at what's broken. And what holds our focus inevitably becomes the object of our faith. Yet think about the absurdity. Mountains don't move by us gawking at their enormity. Bondages don't break by our marveling at the wake of carnage they leave. It's only when we gaze at the beauty of Christ and His Gospel that what's broken can be made whole. Of course, God knows our human tendency to get distracted and become enamored with the obstacles standing in our way. So it's been my experience that from time to time, God will do something extraordinary to capture our attention and get us to see the kingdom solutions He's placed inside us to position us to be the answer for the problems plaguing our world.

I'd only been serving as a lead pastor for just over two years when something pretty unusual happened. Megan and I had recently seen the 2018 film *Instant Family*, which tells the story of a young couple who, feeling a void in their marriage, ultimately stumble into the world of foster care and adoption, where they find themselves speeding from zero to three kids overnight. It was a heartwarming story, and if I'm honest, I did tear up a little in the theater. But having worked for the Indiana Department of Child Services and in different residential treatment centers for children over the years, I had long been familiar with the system, the need and the challenges involved. I had great admiration for those who chose to care for children who'd suffered abuse and neglect, but I was confident that was a path for *them*, not for *me*.

Our youngest child was now a freshman in college, and we were savoring the peace and quiet of our empty nest. This was the moment I'd been looking forward to for about twenty years, and everything was going according to plan. Don't get me wrong. I loved my children to death! I also loved that they were now mostly independent. Everything has its season, and even though Megan had always wanted more kids, I don't think she was hating the sweetness of the season we were in either. Then one Sunday morning, I got up to preach, and midsermon, much to my surprise, these words came out of my mouth: "We're going to be foster parents." It was as though I was having an out-of-body experience! I couldn't believe my own ears, but once the words had left my mouth, there was no getting them back. This scripture immediately came to mind—"When you make a promise to God, don't delay in following through, for God takes no pleasure in fools. Keep all the promises you make to Him" (Ecclesiastes 5:4 NLT).

What was possibly even more peculiar than what had just happened was that I felt a real peace about it. Later, after the service, Megan and I discussed that spontaneous announcement, and it seemed that we were on the same page, and we began the process of becoming foster parents. Several years have passed since then, and we've cared for about a dozen children, some for short periods and some for long. We've adopted the two sweetest, most precious girls in the whole world, and we continue to foster other littles now who we absolutely adore. Megan is still the very best mom I've ever seen.

God has met all our needs, and our hearts are overflowing with joy like never before. Sure, we could be basking in the wholeness of a peaceful empty nest, blissfully ignorant of the brokenness all around us. But we've come to realize that we'd be missing out on the blessing that comes with sharing pieces of our heart and life that can help to make another whole. We can honestly say now that we wouldn't trade this life for anything!

Now, I don't say all this to pat myself on the back but to say that sometimes God's best for our lives can be missed if we're too busy staring at what we think we want. Another way to say this is that the greatest enemy to the plan of God for your life is *your* plan for your life. As I look back now and what I could've missed out on had I stuck to my own plans, I'm so glad that the anointing took over on that Sunday morning and those words spilled out of my mouth before I knew what was happening! What I've found is that when God's desires become your desires, not only do you get your prayers answered, but even the ones you should have prayed get answered too. God is looking for people who'll simply give Him their "yes" to carry out His plans and purposes for their lives. When was the last time you stopped staring at *your* plan for your life long enough to evaluate whether or not it's truly *God's* plan for you? You might be surprised by what He has in store, but I can promise you that you'll never be disappointed.

The American dream is to work hard, save a lot, and then be able to retire, to check out of responsibilities and caretaking and finally care for one person—you! But is that really supposed to be the goal for us as believers? Does our divine purpose have an expiration date? Or are we created with a purpose far greater than a goal of soaking up our golden years, living for ourselves? The idea that we work with the goal to just stop working someday suggests there will come a day where we lose our effectiveness for the kingdom and just become self-focused. But how does that concept reconcile with a world that will always need compassion? With hurting people whose needs don't end? How does a Christ follower prepare for that stage of their life differently from someone who doesn't believe?

I'm reminded of a quote from Eugene Peterson, who said, "Some of us try desperately to hold onto ourselves, to live for ourselves. We look so bedraggled and pathetic doing it, hanging on to the dead branch of a bank account for dear life, afraid to risk ourselves on the untried wings of giving. We don't think we can live generously because we have never tried. But the sooner we start, the better, for we are going to have to give up our lives finally, and the longer we wait, the less time we have for the soaring and swooping life of grace." How sadly and profoundly true!

Maybe the goal should be to focus on kingdom business until the day we're standing on the other side of eternity. Until the day we're looking at the face of Jesus, there's a purpose for us here. And it can't be limited to an age or constrained by our financial situation because God's purpose for us is far bigger than that. What should the next step look like for believers? I'd submit it ought to look just like every step of our lives—to pursue God and His righteousness and to trust Him to care for the rest. Interestingly, the Hebrew word for personal righteousness is the word *tzedakah* (צדקה). And it just so happens that the Hebrew word for outward justice is also tzedakah. See, biblically speaking, our personal righteousness cannot be separated from our public works of justice. The inward always spills over into the outward. What God has joined together, we aren't meant to separate. Likewise, the goal isn't just to get to heaven but to get heaven into us, and once we have the King's heart, the kingdom will flow out of us without end.

Your feet will ultimately move in the direction of your faith, but your faith will either be enlarged or reduced by where you place your focus. If you set your sights on the things of this life, with its temporal rewards and consequences, it can be easy to feel assured that you've done enough. As you compare the level of your investment into God's kingdom with other people you attend church alongside, it's only natural that you'd feel pleased with how your life measures up if you've done even a modicum of good in service to the Lord. But when you set your sights on eternity, with the immensity of its everlasting rewards and consequences, it's unthinkable that you could just sit back and rest on your laurels. I'm sure no one arrives in heaven and thinks to themselves, *Boy, I wish I hadn't given so much of my money in support of missions during my brief time on earth!* Or, *You know, I should've spent less time serving others! It would've been better if I'd just left it to the professionals to tell people about Jesus.* The reality is, in that moment, the full weight of your contribution will be measured, and you'll stand in full agreement with the verdict rendered by Jesus as He judges your works, knowing that all His judgments are perfect and just. The question to ask yourself now is, how will you feel about it all when you stare into His eyes?

This problem of focus and staring at the wrong thing(s) has plagued us from the very beginning. God told Adam and Eve they could eat from all the trees of the garden, except one. So what did the serpent do? He got them to focus on the one they couldn't eat from. God calls us to an abundance mindset to see all we have, while evil tries to get us to focus on what we lack. Pastors and leaders, we have to stop seeing who isn't in the room and what isn't happening yet. The enemy understands he can't stop you, so instead, what does he do? He distracts you. The focus on what isn't will only continue to keep you from what is. The key to the more God has in store is gratitude for all that He's already provided and to steward each moment by giving your "yes" to Jesus. As you are faithful with the little He's entrusted to you, He'll bestow His favor upon you by entrusting you with even greater responsibility for His kingdom (Luke 16:10 NLT).

In this life, we can become discouraged when we see sinners succeeding and evil people prospering. We can become disheartened when our obedience isn't met with instant blessing. But when our eyes are fixed on eternity and we have a right view of God, we're guided by a confidence in His perfect and righteous judgments—that every injustice will be accounted for, every wrong will be made right, and every act of faithful devotion to Him will be rewarded. When Jesus returns, every celebrity will be nameless, every millionaire will be penniless, and every politician will be powerless. But the bride of Christ will be known, named, rich, and powerful beyond anyone's wildest imagination. When we live for that day, it becomes a whole lot easier to live for this one. When we stare at the Savior, we're reminded that every choice has costs and consequences. There's a hell yet to be plundered and a heaven yet to be populated. So if faith is your currency, go all in! Minimal investment will never yield maximum results, but believers who sacrifice as if they take God at His word that He truly is the Rewarder He says He is won't be disappointed when they stand before Him at the coming Judgment Seat of Christ.

REFLECTIONS

1. The pursuit of the American dream to work with the goal to just stop working someday and check out of our responsibilities and caretaking suggests there'll come a day where we lose our effectiveness for the kingdom and just become self-focused. How do you reconcile that concept with a world that will always need compassion? With hurting people whose needs don't end?

2. How might a Christ follower prepare for that stage of their life differently from someone who doesn't believe? Does our divine purpose have an expiration date? Or are we created with a purpose far greater than a goal of soaking up our golden years, living for ourselves?

3. When was the last time you stopped staring at *your* plan for your life long enough to evaluate whether or not it's truly *God's* plan for you? How can you be sure you're serving the Lord in all His plans for your life and you haven't instead begun expecting Him to serve you in your plans?

4. Do you live with the goal of just getting to heaven, or do you desperately desire to get heaven into you in order to have the King's heart, that the kingdom would flow out of you without end?

5. Read 1 Corinthians 3:8–15 and 2 Corinthians 5:9–10. It's an incredibly humbling thought that the God of all creation would choose to partner with us to accomplish His purposes here on the earth and that our efforts will have an eternal impact. What an awesome responsibility! Your faith will either be enlarged

or reduced by where you place your focus. When you set your sights on eternity with a heaven to gain and a hell to shun, how do you think your investment of time, talents, and treasures will be measured and judged? What seemingly good things can steal away your attention and possibly cause you to miss out on greater things God was calling you to do?

6. Take a moment to consider what it will be like to stand alone before the King of kings in heaven one day. If your good deeds (done in obedience to Jesus) are like gems in a crown (1 Corinthians 9:25, Philippians 4:1, Revelation 4:10 NLT), what will you have to present to Him?

CHAPTER 11

THE MORTICIANS

When we finally arrive at the scene of Christ's burial, there are two characters who take center stage—two secret disciples of Jesus who emerge from the shadows and ultimately serve as His morticians. The first was Joseph of Arimathea. Luke records that he was a good and righteous man; a member of the Jewish high council who didn't agree with the decision and actions of the other religious leaders (Luke 23:50–51 NLT). While the rest of the disciples were hiding in fear and confusion, Joseph of Arimathea acted with incredible courage and devotion. Mark tells us that "As evening approached, Joseph of Arimathea took a risk and went to Pilate and asked for Jesus' body. Joseph bought a long sheet of linen cloth. Then he took Jesus' body down from the cross, wrapped it in the cloth, and laid it in a tomb that had been carved out of the rock. Then he rolled a stone in front of the entrance" (Mark 15:42–43, 46 NLT).

Joseph had, in effect, just put a target on his own back because asking Pilate for the body was a public declaration of his love for Jesus. Joseph's identity as an undercover disciple would no longer be a secret. When he could've just stayed in the shadows, Joseph instead stepped into the middle of a legal and political drama, the very drama that put the rest of the disciples on the run and into hiding. In one daring move, Joseph risked everything—his wealth, his reputation, his power, and even his life. As a member of the inner council of the Sanhedrin, it was his peers who'd just pressured Pilate to try Jesus for treason and have Him hanged on a cross. But Joseph loved his Lord too much to let His body rot on the cross or be thrown into some shallow public grave along with a group of common criminals. With a heart of worship, he gave the Messiah his tomb. With a heart of love, he ensured his Lord was buried with honor.

Like the others, Joseph of Arimathea had no clue what God was doing. He didn't know what the future would hold, let alone that the worst thing to have ever happened—the death of Jesus—would become the best thing to ever happen. This Joseph had the same questions, doubts, and fears as the rest. In that instant, it seemed like all was lost, and nothing made sense. Yet despite the confusion and terror of the moment, Joseph of Arimathea would take a bold and faithful stand. Isn't it tempting for us to think that we'd have more peace, courage, and obedience in life if we could know what God was up to all the time? If only we knew why we had to go through that sickness, why we had to lose that job, why we had to endure that marriage that ended in disastrous betrayal. If only we knew, then we would sleep more peacefully, live more obediently, and act more courageously. Or so we tell ourselves.

We all experience moments when life just doesn't seem to make sense. We all hit those times where who God says He is seems to contradict what He's allowed to come into our lives. In those moments, it can be tempting to question the heart, plan, and power of God. But there's great danger in allowing ourselves to doubt His character because it's then that we stop running to God for help and instead retreat to a place of spiritual isolation, paralyzed by our questions, doubts, and fears. Like Adam and Eve before us, when we rely on our finite understanding, we often invite in the very destruction that God, in His infinite wisdom, was trying to keep out.

The fact of the matter is that no matter how deep and robust your theological understanding is, there'll always be mystery in your life. God reveals to us what we need to know in order to follow Him by faith, but He doesn't promise to reveal all He knows or all He's doing. Waiting seasons can be some of the most difficult times in our lives, but they don't have to be. These are the moments and seasons when God issues us a holy invitation into rest—not the kind of rest marked by the absence of activity but a rest that's found in the absence of control. Our minds don't find peace when we figure it all out but when we trust the one who understands all things, rules over all things, and withholds no good thing from our lives.

Joseph had no clue what would result from his courageous act of worshipful love, no idea that his tomb of death would sit in human history as a symbol of life pointing to the redemptive grace and resurrection power of Almighty God. Neither do we have any idea of what God will do in and through us as we act in the courage of expectant faith that lovingly trusts the plan of God that we cannot understand. See, when we try to approach life like a puzzle to be solved or a map to be read in advance, we live in a constant state of unrest and dissatisfaction. But like Joseph, when we make peace with the tensions that exist between the perfect will of God clearly communicated in scripture and the imperfect status of our circumstances, our obedience won't be bound by the limitations of our understanding.

In addition to Joseph of Arimathea, the other secret disciple who resurfaces at Christ's burial is Nicodemus—a wealthy Pharisee best known for secretly meeting Jesus at night because he feared being seen by other Jewish leaders. The story of Nicodemus only appears in three chapters of the Bible in the Gospel of John. In chapter 3, he only secretly visits Jesus to seek information. This is the scene when Jesus famously tells Nicodemus that he must be born again. In chapter 7, Nicodemus speaks up in Jesus's defense when the Jewish leaders want to seize Him. And by the time we arrive at chapter 19, Nicodemus is no longer intimidated by the Pharisees, and he takes physical action, helping to remove Jesus from the cross. Each time

Nicodemus is mentioned in the Bible, he speaks and acts bolder for Christ, and by the time of Jesus's crucifixion, Nicodemus had grown bold enough to publicly reveal what he now believed. Some accounts even mention Nicodemus's gifts and actions helping the early church grow amidst persecution.

Together, Joseph and Nicodemus brought the body of Jesus to the new garden tomb, along with about seventy-five pounds of perfumed ointment to prepare the body for proper burial (John 19:38–42 NLT). As Josh McDowell states in his article, *Burial Details of the Resurrection of Christ*, "Starting at Jesus' feet, the two men would have wrapped Jesus' body in linen cloth, placing aromatic spices mixed with a gummy substance called myrrh between the folds. Jewish custom dictated that Jesus' torso be wrapped to His armpits. His preparers would have then placed Jesus' arms straight alongside His body, before wrapping more linen cloth around Him, to the neck. A separate cloth was wrapped around His head. As the gummy myrrh would have adhered so closely to Jesus' body, it would have been difficult by this point for anyone to remove the linen cloth. And yet the Gospels record that the burial cloths were found in the empty burial tomb—neatly folded!"

The reality is that the morticians were essential to the resurrection story in that someone had to bury the body before it could be raised by the power of God. Someone had to apply the gummy myrrh and the linen cloths that would become part of the convincing evidence left at the scene when Peter and John arrived at the empty tomb, along with Mary Magdalene. Now, I don't know about you, but if I was signing up for a role in the Gospel narrative, this definitely isn't the one I'd have chosen! And who knows, maybe that thought occurred to these guys too. But I believe Joseph and Nicodemus had grown tired of trying to be the person everyone else thought they should be. And when they finally stepped out of the shadows and into the spotlight, this was exactly the role they needed to begin walking in the fullness of who God called them to be.

Did Joseph's family try to keep him quiet about his devotion to following Jesus? Had Nicodemus been feeling the weight of others' expectations to maintain his class and social status rather than risking it all to serve Christ? We'll never know the answer to those questions on this side of heaven, but we can certainly assume it wasn't an easy choice for them to go against the grain of culture and fight against their own flesh that was telling them to do the safe and sensible thing. You know, whether it's by the trappings of wealth, the expectations of family, the pressures of society, or the limitations brought on by your past decisions, the hardest person to be is always the one someone else wants you to be. True freedom is found only when you embrace the reality of who God made you to be and what He called you to do. It's then alone that you become the most real version of yourself, congruent in thought and deed with what your spirit bears witness to at the deepest levels of your being.

Christian leader, this is why it's imperative that we make formation in Christ the priority, so we don't keep on producing Christians who are ambiguous about their identity, or who are indistinguishable in their character from nonbelievers. In our zeal to reach the lost, may we not fail at discipling the found—at drawing the Josephs and Nicodemuses in our care out of the shadows of their fears and limitations to step into the fullness of discipleship in Christ. It's incumbent upon us to teach the difference between what's a part of our identity and what's simply a part of our story.

People need to be told that their personality isn't their destiny; it's merely their tendency. That failure doesn't define a man's résumé. It merely represents an opportunity for growth once we get past all our "that's just the way I am" excuses. That who we become isn't about the traits that we have; it's what we decide to do with them that determines the ceiling of our potential. The fact is that God can use *anyone* to the extent that they believe it possible and are willing to be conformed to the image of Christ. But how can they believe this unless they're told?

When we successfully disciple those in our care to pattern their lives after Jesus, we'll inevitably replicate healthy disciples with an others-first mentality. Serving even when they hurt. Giving even when they lack. Praying for others even when they feel distant from God themselves. Why? Because they understand that what they sow into the life of others, God will cause them to reap in their own life. They've found the secret that when they refresh others, they themselves will be refreshed. And they've embraced the mystery that it truly is better to give than it is to receive.

These were the things that marked the lives of first-century disciples, and they are the things that should characterize the life of any believer whose identity has been formed in Christ and whose life has been patterned after Him. We suffer to get well, we surrender to win, we die to live, and we find fullness by giving ourselves away. This is the kind of life that true discipleship demands because this is what it takes to become like Jesus. These are the kinds of people God desires to elevate into places of leadership because the reality is when the leaders God desires are leading, then the people God loves are flourishing.

There's a direct correlation between the well-being of the people of God and the health of the leadership in the church of God. When a man or woman steps into the fullness of who they're called to be and humbly does the hard work no one else sees, it always sets the stage for God to reveal Himself to people in ways both big and small. Just as what Joseph and Nicodemus did in secret played an integral part in setting the stage for the public moment the stone was rolled away from the tomb, the Lord is looking for some modern-day morticians who won't care who gets the credit so long as God gets the glory.

Are you finished letting your past overshadow your purpose for one moment longer? Are you done trying to fit the mold of what others expect you to be? Perhaps you are that man or woman. Maybe now is your time to step out of the shadows and into the identity and purpose of God in this chapter of the story He's writing. May we never consider it the mark of a healthy life to be well adjusted to an unhealthy culture. To that end, before we can expect to replicate spiritual health, we must first put to death what we've learned from being exposed to toxic environments. I've found that perhaps the greatest enemy to our freedom and progress is a familiar mindset. Simply put, we can't be brought into the new that God has for us until we break out of old paradigms that are too small for what God has in mind.

REFLECTIONS

1. Life won't always make sense to us, and there will always be an element of mystery to our experiences in this world. When we resist this reality, we become plagued by unrest and find ourselves dissatisfied. Are you content to rest in the mystery of the Lord or do you feel the need to constantly try to answer the question of *why*? In moments or seasons when you find it difficult to understand the will of God, what helps or hinders your ability to obey Him?

2. Swimming upstream against the current of culture that tells us to do the safe and sensible thing is an ongoing struggle. The expectations of family and pressures of society to be who someone else wants us to be tend to run contrary to who God made us to be and what He's called us to do. Like Joseph and Nicodemus, God will often call us to step into roles that are meant for supernatural enhancement but not necessarily for natural enjoyment. How have you experienced this dynamic in your life? As you've been faithful to steward these opportunities, how has God elevated you and given you greater responsibility for His kingdom?

3. Jesus has commissioned us to replicate healthy disciples with an others-first mentality—serving even when they hurt, giving even when they lack, and praying for others even when they feel distant from God. We suffer to get well, we surrender to win, we die to live, and we find fullness by giving ourselves away. This is the kind of life that true discipleship demands because this is what it takes to become like Jesus. These are the kinds of people God desires to elevate into places of leadership because

the reality is when the leaders God desires are leading, then the people God loves are flourishing. The reality is the church is only as strong as our discipleship is healthy. Who are you discipling? Who's discipling you? What results are you seeing replicated?

4. Healthy spirituality won't emerge from becoming well-adjusted to an unhealthy culture. What familiar mindsets have you learned from toxic environments that need to be broken in your life?

CHAPTER 12

THE GARDENER

At long last, we come to Resurrection Day—the pinnacle moment of the Gospels. The tomb is now empty. Death, hell, and the grave are now defeated. The risen Savior would soon be going to prepare a place for the sons and daughters of God. The King of kings would ascend to His throne where He'll reign for all eternity. Everything we enjoy today and all that we have to look forward to in our tomorrows hinges on the significance of this moment. Truly, this was the greatest day in the history of the world—one that I believe is fully deserving of our most unabashed and exuberant celebration. But sometimes, in all our zeal and excitement, I'd submit that we can rush toward the sublime miracle of resurrection and, in doing so, miss out on subtle moments of revelation Jesus shares with us along the way.

We don't need to ascend to the heights of heaven to tap into the revelation Christ gives. If that were the case, He would've simply taken us out of this world the moment we were saved. Instead, what scripture shows us is that the Lord uses the common things of this world to reveal the deeper truths of the kingdom to our hearts. His first appearance after rising from the dead is no exception. Made plain to us in the setting of the story itself, not far from the stony hill of crucifixion and death, we learn from John the beloved that Jesus's tomb (the one that belonged to Joseph of Arimathea) was located in a garden. And it's there that Christ first appeared to one of His most loyal followers who had come to mourn.

In order to fully capture what happens here, we need to piece together the writings of Mark and John to create a unified picture in our minds. To begin, Mark gives us not only the identity of this follower but also their background. He writes, "When Jesus rose early on the first day of the week, He appeared first to Mary Magdalene, out of whom He had driven seven demons" (Mark 16:9 NIV). Mary Magdalene, who would become the first messenger of the Gospel, wasn't too dissimilar from the place where Jesus now found her—the new life that God was producing in her not far removed from her dark past of demonic torment and control. She was a firsthand witness to Jesus's crucifixion and burial. Now also to His resurrection, though she wouldn't yet know it. It was through her eyes that Christ would choose to reveal the full plan of God now complete. The story she had to tell wasn't one of mere historical or even miraculous events but one of personal encounter. Jesus had found her in her darkest place, and now, as one who walked in the light (1 John 1:5–7 NIV), she had become the embodiment of faithful devotion.

Sideswept by intense grief, however, Mary didn't realize who was standing before her. Through her haze of despair, she heard the man ask her, "'Woman, why are you crying? Who is it you are looking for?' Thinking He was the gardener, she said, 'Sir, if you have carried Him away, tell me where you have put Him, and I will get Him.' Jesus said to her, 'Mary.' She turned toward Him and cried out in Aramaic, 'Rabboni!' (which means 'Teacher')" (John 20:15–16 NIV). Time and again, we've heard that in John's resurrection story, Mary Magdalene was confused outside the tomb, thinking Jesus was the gardener. A logical mistake. Or a prophetic mistake. Or a beautiful mistake. Or perhaps not a mistake at all. Mary was absolutely correct—Jesus *is* the Gardener who performs the earthy and intimate work of tending our souls.

In his Gospel account, John interweaves many strands of creation and re-creation to tell the story of the incarnation, death, and resurrection of Jesus. He begins by evoking the garden of Genesis: "In the beginning ..." (John 1:1 NASB) and ends with "Now in the place where He was crucified there was a garden, and in the garden was a new tomb" (John 19:41 NASB). Here, we see incarnation, death, and resurrection are linked with re-creation. A garden was the place wherein we fell, and now a garden is where the greatest work of our redemption would begin. Mary had encountered the Gardener who she knew brings forth new life from the dirt and filth of our sinful lives. When Mary heard her name spoken, she knew. Only Jesus says her name like that; there was no mistaking it. As she turned and beheld the kind smile and piercing eyes of the Son of God, there would now be no convincing her that she hadn't met with a man believed to be dead. Through this encounter with the Gardener, Mary would discover the beautiful Gospel truth that intimacy with God ultimately dislodges our doubts and destroys the limitations of our logic.

One of the things I love most about Jesus is that He doesn't wait for broken things to be made beautiful before He blesses them. Rather, He seeks out those who the world counts out, and somehow in the soil of these flawed vessels, He cultivates something holy. The Gardener is constantly unearthing those things we've buried deep down—our painful past, our secret sins, and our dead dreams—in order to bring forth healing, forgiveness, and restoration. It's what He does, and still today, He's bringing beauty from ashes and transforming graves into gardens. Mary's life is a portrait of God's power at work in us "to will and to act in order to fulfill His good purpose" (Philippians 2:13 NIV). Her story reminds us that Jesus isn't looking for worthy people whose lives are already cleaned up to carry His message and do His work, because no such person exists. Instead, He's simply looking for those who'll reject the trappings of dead religion and allow the hand of God to touch their dirty lives. Gardening, as it turns out, is an essential element of Christ's relationship with us. Tilling, sowing, pruning, and watering are integral to the way the Lord leads His people. He cultivates through grace-rich soil, creating the conditions for His people to flourish, that we might nourish others.

In terms of leadership, the lesson here is simple and straightforward—look for the dirt and get involved. We can't do life with people and expect to somehow keep our hands clean. If we aren't intentional about working with dirty people and in dirty places, we limit God's ability to cultivate something beautiful through our lives and ministries, because we aren't stewarding the same raw materials Jesus did that ultimately produced a Mary Magdalene–type testimony. The kingdom of God is about more than what we grow; it's about developing the seeds of greatness in others. Relationships are key to the will of God, and those who He brings into our life are more than a means to an end. They are a gift in and of themselves. When we steward relationships well, we maximize others' God-given potential to blossom, as well as our own.

Although Adam and Eve's deception had turned their garden into a wilderness that separated them from the one who walked with them in the cool of day (Genesis 3:8 NIV), Jesus's victory turned His wilderness into a garden that restored our fellowship with the Almighty. When life is hard, opportunities dry up, or relationships feel barren, we often feel like we're in the desert, as if God has disappeared. But in reality, the desert is the place where God lives and speaks. Think about it; it was in the desert that God spoke to Abraham, Moses, Isaiah, and even Jesus. So rather than asking God *when* you can get out of the desert, why not ask Him *what* you can get out of the desert? The stony places like Golgotha where few signs of life exist are often the vehicle God uses to lead us to the beauty of new life springing up in the place of the garden tomb.

The wilderness seasons of life certainly hold immense promise when we lean into God's purpose for them, but they can also pose imminent danger when we lack patience. It's then that we can feel panicked, causing us to look for a means of escape before God's time comes for us to exit. Fear can cause us to force open doors outside of God's timing. We may think we're simply speeding God's plan along, but we fail to realize that the doors we open with our own gifting must continue to be held open in our own strength. Sadly, when we make our own way, we'll have only an illusion of influencing the world, but when we wait for what God has in store, we'll actually be able to accomplish it. I know how difficult it can feel to remain in hard places, but I've learned from experience to do it anyway. These seasons form us. And like Golgotha, we'll never know the potential of the garden if we don't first trust God with what He's developing in the darkness of the grave. Remember, God always equips those He calls and makes fruitful the dreams He plants in our hearts. Our job is obedience, and when we take care of our part, the Lord takes care of His part, which is the outcome.

Like Mary Magdalene, we need tender and responsive hearts of repentance that allow wrong things to die so that right things can live. We need ears that hear the Gardener's voice calling us into encounter. However, in seasons when we find it hard to discern His voice, we mustn't turn to other voices or settle for the wisdom of man. Instead, when we struggle to *hear* the Gardener, we need to be reminded to *read* Him. One of the Hebrew words we translate as "garden" is the word *pardes* (פַּרְדֵּס). I find it incredible that in rabbinic teaching, this word is also used to describe the study of scripture, using the acronym "PRDS" (since ancient Hebrew writing only used consonants). Here's what each letter represents—P (*P'shat*): the simple meaning; R (*Remez*): the implied meaning; D (*Drash*): the deeper meaning; and S (*Sod*): the hidden meaning. Because the first letters of these Hebrew words create the word *pardes*, it's said that studying the Bible is like being in God's garden—not the barren garden from the fall of Adam but the lush garden from the resurrected Christ where we, like Mary Magdalene, can have a personal encounter with the Gardener Himself. The depth of that encounter is entirely up to us. Will we settle for the simple on the surface, explore what's implied, dig deeply, or perhaps even uncover revelation that was previously hidden from our understanding that holds immense power to transform?

One of the most amazing realities about the Christian faith is that Jesus is truly alive in every person who receives the Seed, and His desire is to increase, producing good fruit from our lives. But just as seeds can't grow if you fail to water them, the same is true in the spirit. If what's sown in the kingdom isn't watered, there can be no growth. Yet the church has increasingly become known by its factions—with certain denominational streams being known by their affection for the Spirit of God and others being known for their devotion to the Word of God. However, I believe we're living in a day and age when we're about to witness the fulfillment of Christ's words to the Samaritan woman in John 4, as He declared to her that "a time is coming and has now come when the true worshipers will worship the Father in the Spirit and in truth, for they are the kind of worshipers the Father seeks" (John 4:23 NIV). The kind of worship Jesus speaks of here has both already come and not yet been fully realized.

As we see in the text, Jesus had just left Judea, where the Pharisees took issue with Him and His disciples for the vast number of people they were baptizing into The Way. He was headed to Galilee, where Judeans felt the people were far too lax in their observance of proper religious ritual. Jesus's remarks to the woman at Jacob's well in Samaria hold prophetic power that points to the merging of these two streams and the outpouring of living water that will result as God's people come together to worship Him in Spirit and in truth. No longer will people of the Word be without the saturation of the Spirit's presence, and no more will people of the Spirit be without the richness of the Word and the deep rooting of discipleship. The reformation God is bringing to His church will include both to bring us into maturity, and I'm convinced both will be required in order for this next move of God to be sustained.

The church of Jesus Christ must become lovers of both Word

and Spirit. As these two operate together, they'll usher in a revival that runs as deep as it does wide, resulting in not only unprecedented salvations but an unmatched supply of workers being sent out into the harvest fields. This will be an era marked not by the counting of hands raised but by the counting of feet that follow in the path of true discipleship. Inflated numbers that make us feel successful at face value will no longer suffice because that which doesn't cost us anything ultimately will be revealed as not being worth anything. That which is fake will fail, and only that which multiplies will be able to be sustained.

Bible-teaching churches and Spirit-led churches will no longer be pitted against one another but will instead glean from one another for the benefit of the overall body. The old saying is true: "If you have all Word, you dry up. If you have all Spirit, you blow up. If you have Word and Spirit, you grow up." The future of the church will need to be both sound theologically and deep experientially. The fullness of the true Gospel can only be reflected by a people who love both God's Word and the presence of His Spirit. These are the ones who grab hold of the vine with both hands, whose lives produce fruit—a harvest of righteousness for God's glory. We simply cannot afford to pass the baton of leadership to a generation that hasn't been mentored in how to steward both sound doctrine as well as dynamic spiritual gifting and power. To do so would be nothing short of reckless.

To some, this period of reformation will feel like the church is starting over because it'll look unlike anything we've witnessed before, but in reality, we're just being pruned. God likes to prune, and He always prunes back to love. The teaching many of us have heard on pruning usually addresses it on a personal level. But I'd like to suggest that God also prunes on a macro level with His church. Jesus said, "I am the true vine, and my Father is the gardener. He cuts off every branch in me that bears no fruit, while every branch that does bear fruit He prunes so that it will be even more fruitful" (John 15:1–2 NIV). The word used here for "prune" (καθαίρω, kathairō) simply means "to clear or cut away what is unproductive." And scripture tells us the purpose for this pruning is to "bear more fruit." As we look at the big picture with pruning and the kingdom of God, we first need to understand that while God's Word never changes, we must continue to grow and change. And this must happen on a corporate level as well. In fact, this is the whole purpose of leadership gifts in the church—until we all come into the unity of the faith, growing up into Christ, having His knowledge and His maturity (Ephesians 4:11–16 NLT). We're not there yet, but Jesus is building His church, and He won't stop until she looks like Him!

Each move of God brings in a fresh wave of the Spirit, and the understanding of our life in Christ is upgraded. In the aftermath of the deconstruction movement, I see God raising up "pruners" with burning hearts who have the gifting to discern the times and see what's good and what needs to be cut away from our current understanding. A freshness and vitality is being restored to the church. A new sound is being released from heaven that's producing an explosion of new creativity and healthy increase of fruitfulness. The pruning of the Lord isn't something to fear or resist. In fact, the end result will be a general feeling among God's people of joy and freedom, like they're coming alive for the very first time—hearts burning afresh with heaven's passion and desire. Pruning brings increase. That means something gets added. There's increase and growth in the experiential knowledge of God. This higher heavenly freedom in the sense of a fuller revelation of our identity—of Christ and Him crucified in us (1 Corinthians 2:2 NIV).

Rather than destroying what was, pruning builds on the foundation. One thing we need to realize in this is that although each move brings us up higher, it doesn't mean that the move in a previous generation somehow missed it or they were disobedient. No, they were the frontier of the kingdom on earth, the fruitful branches of their time. But to stay where the church was five hundred years ago would clearly be unproductive and unfruitful for us. God's kingdom is a living thing, ever expanding and always advancing.

So we must advance with it. Imagine I showed you a plot of land covered with weeds and said, "I'm going to turn this into a garden." If I showed up and pulled up all the weeds, you wouldn't look at that barren plot of dirt and say, "Wow, what a beautiful garden!" Of course not. See, while the pruning of the Gardener will naturally involve the displacing and disposing of some things, it also includes the replacing and replanting of other things. It's not just about uprooting what's toxic, as important as that is. It's also, by God's grace, setting our minds, hearts, and lives on the good things God has called us to. We must both let go of what was as well as step into what is.

The words of the prophet Isaiah resound in my spirit as I consider this new era in church history—"Forget the former things; do not dwell on the past. See, I am doing a new thing! Now it springs up; do you not perceive it? I am making a way in the wilderness and streams in the wasteland" (Isaiah 43:18–19 NIV). As the church steps into this new season, the message of Good News must remain the same, but our methods need to adapt to the ever-changing landscape as we prepare for harvest. I believe a singular focus on souls will cause streams to merge together in the Spirit and denominational dams to be demolished. Fears of what could be lost in terms of our ideological identity will be washed away by the hopes of what could be gained as we join efforts as one unified kingdom for the glory of God. As our hearts are forged together with the burning desire to see another great move of God in the earth, the bride of Christ will shine her light more radiantly than ever before as a beacon for our Bridegroom's soon return.

God is bringing together leaders who'll co-labor to see cities, regions, and nations transformed. When we learn to gather around the person of Christ and not merely doctrine about Him, a unity will emerge that's founded in mutual submission to the Lord Jesus. Leaders who may not always speak the same language in terms of background and ministry flow but prioritize a mutual honor and partnership will release an unprecedented anointing that brings transformation. As we run with others who want to run and build with others who want to build, we'll discover the multiplied effectiveness that's possible through collaboration, and we'll produce exponentially more fruit than we could dream of. The reformers God is raising up in this hour are those who love a trench more than talent and value the field more than fame. They know who they are and who they aren't, where they're strong and where they need to be strengthened. They're able to defer to each other and promote one another without competition, understanding God has created us to be stronger when linked together because only then can we fulfill our ultimate purpose as the body, completing the image of Immanuel, God with us.

The church God is building is one where the broken can be put back together. A church where those who are hurt can be healed. A church filled with sons and daughters pursuing every righteous assignment the Lord has for them. It's a powerful church marked by those who desire to live a sanctified life. Brothers and sisters who call on the Lord with pure hearts, ready for the Master to use them for good works. This is a generation like those we read about in the New Testament, who are called to bring the Gospel to a secularized world by means of demonstration and not merely conversation. Seeds of revival are beginning to bud in these young ones, but they must be cultivated in atmospheres of awakening where Spirit and truth are mutually revered.

In order for the next generation to blossom into the fullness of their calling, they need to be provided deep soil. They need to be immersed in deep community, deep truth, and deep spirituality that's rich with presence and purpose. Carrying an insatiable spiritual thirst, Gen Z holds immense potential to produce a multiplied harvest for the kingdom of God. We who belong to a previous generation have been given the assignment of tending to the soil, ridding it of rocks and weeds, sowing good seed, and keeping it saturated with the Spirit's presence. What a humbling thought that we get to partner with the Gardener as He brings new life to a once devastated landscape. What an exciting opportunity we have to re-envision a stronger, more complete spiritual family where people can come to encounter the risen Savior for themselves and then run in unison with the message of Good News for all to hear! May we not resist the pruning of the Gardener out of our fear of change, but may we trust Him to do what He does best. Golgotha is the goal, but it's not the end. It's merely a gateway to the verdant garden Christ has prepared in advance for us as we walk in restored relationship with our Creator.

Perhaps the apostle Paul described it best, saying, "This resurrection life you received from God is not a timid, grave-tending life. It's adventurously expectant, greeting God with a childlike 'What's next, Papa?' God's Spirit touches our spirits and confirms who we really are. We know who He is, and we know who we are: Father and children. And we know we are going to get what's coming to us—an unbelievable inheritance! We go through exactly what Christ goes through. If we go through the hard times with Him, then we're certainly going to go through the good times with Him" (Romans 8:15–17 MSG). Truly, our greatest days lie ahead!

REFLECTIONS

1. Just as with Mary Magdalene, Jesus is looking for people who'll reject the trappings of dead religion and allow the hand of God to touch their dirty lives and cultivate something holy. Take a moment to testify about some things the Gardener unearthed from the depths of your heart and how He's brought healing, forgiveness, and restoration. In what ways has He brought beauty from ashes and transformed your grave into a garden?

2. In what ways are you being intentional about sourcing and stewarding the same raw materials Jesus used to produce a Mary Magdalene–type testimony? In other words, how do you make it a point to associate with sinners, rather than hiding out in the safety and comfort of your Christian bubble? Do you find in yourself an aversion to what's dirty, or are you drawn to it? Why is that?

3. In the wilderness seasons of life, do you find yourself lacking patience? Have you tried to force open doors as a means of escape outside of God's timing to exit? What are some potential negative outcomes that can result from relying on our own gifting to make a way for ourselves?

4. What did you think about the idea that studying the Bible is like being in God's garden? Do you find yourself most often settling for the simple on the surface? Exploring what's implied? Digging deeper? Or, as you've read and reread familiar portions of scripture, have you ever uncovered revelation that was previously hidden from your understanding? Does the notion of having a personal encounter with the Gardener Himself excite you? How

does inviting the Lord to accompany you in your reading of the Word transform you and your experience of the truth?

5. As you think about the saturation of the Spirit's presence and the deep rooting of discipleship working together to bring a greater strength and unity to the church, what barriers come to mind that are preventing different streams from collaborating more effectively? What unproductive aspects of the body do you see the Lord pruning? What might increased fruitfulness look like?

CONCLUSION

THE GOAL

Although often misunderstood by His disciples at the time, Jesus always had a goal in mind—someplace He was trying to lead them to or something He was wanting to develop in them. In Matthew 17, we see that Jesus had taken His three closest disciples, Peter, James, and John, up the Mount of Transfiguration, where they'd be witness to extraordinary glory. Scripture records that "As the men watched, Jesus' appearance was transformed so that His face shone like the sun, and His clothes became as white as light. Suddenly, Moses and Elijah appeared and began talking with Jesus" (Matthew 17:2–3 NLT). Can you imagine how shocking this must've been to the disciples? I'm sure they could hardly believe their eyes! In the very next verse, however, we see Peter's reaction, which clearly missed what Jesus had intended. It says, "Peter exclaimed, 'Lord, it's wonderful for us to be here! If you want, I'll make three shelters as memorials—one for You, one for Moses, and one for Elijah'" (Matthew 17:4 NLT). Can you imagine how bizarre it must've been to Jesus that Peter's response to what he'd just seen would be to build a museum?

I don't know about you, but I can find myself sometimes looking at New Testament passages like this and thinking, *How could they have been so clueless? How did they miss it so badly?* Then I step back and realize how often we too have been clueless, how badly we still miss it, even with the Word of God to show us the way. I mean, just think, the greatest victory of all time was secured at Golgotha. Incomparable glory would be displayed at the resurrection. Yet how many have treated the cross as something to be memorialized rather than the place where we're transformed so our lives can shine like Jesus? How often have we missed the goal? The crucifixion wasn't the final stroke of heaven's divine paintbrush in the portrait of God's redemptive story to be displayed in the museum of a church building. It was the beginning of restored fellowship with the Father and the coronation of His kingdom come here on the earth.

Thankfully, in order to understand the goal God has in mind, we need not look any further than His Word. In Hebrews, chapter 13, He makes it as plain as can be. There we read, "Jesus suffered and died outside the city gates to make His people holy by means of His own blood. So let us go out to Him, outside the camp, and bear the disgrace He bore. For this world is not our permanent home; we are looking forward to a home yet to come" (Hebrews 13:12–14 NLT). There it is, encapsulated in these three verses—God's goal: past, present, and future. We see what Jesus did and why. We see what we're supposed to do as a result. And finally, we see the eternal perspective we're meant to have in preparation for our future home. I think John Piper brings clarity in his summation of this passage saying the point is loud and clear: "Christians, move toward need, not comfort." This is the radical call of Christ issued from the place of the skull. This is the way of the upside down kingdom where the last are first, the weak are strong, and those who lose their life find it. The point is to go with Jesus outside the camp of comfort, familiarity, and security to where the needs are, to stop trying to make our lives paradise on earth and instead move toward the joy that's set before us in Zion, the city that is to come.

God knew we needed more than an explanation of the Gospel we could understand. We needed an example of the Gospel we could follow. So, not only did He give us Jesus, but He also gave us the New Testament church to pattern our lives after. Their daily devotion, selfless sacrifice, fearless faith, and laid down lives show us what it's supposed to look like to truly follow Jesus. And if we're going to do the same, it's going to require a shift from being an apathetic audience to becoming an activated army, from being entertained consumers to becoming activated contributors who minister the Gospel and demonstrate the kingdom. A remnant is rising in preparation for Christ's return. You'll see Him soon. The best and worst decisions you can ever make in life will be the ones you make with that final moment in mind.

In light of that fateful moment when man will stand face-to-face with their Creator and Judge, scripture urgently warns us, "Do not merely listen to the Word, and so deceive yourselves. Do what it says" (James 1:22 NIV). The self-deception that James speaks of here relates to an inappropriate response to the truth of God's Word that's meant to change us. We can sit in church for years and even read the Bible from cover to cover, but unless we put its truth into practice, we deceive ourselves. Self-deception is frighteningly common among religious people who store up the truth of God in their minds, assuming that's what being a good Christian is all about. But scripture wasn't given merely to produce Bible scholars and theologians. It was given "so that the servant of God may be thoroughly equipped for every good work" (2 Timothy 3:17 NIV). When Christ returns, the question of your life won't be about what you know. It'll be about what you did with what you know, and the only thing that will count, according to God's Word, is faith expressing itself through love (Galatians 5:6 NIV).

Christian, whether you realize it or not, each of us will stand before the throne of God to give an account for our lives during our short stay on earth (Romans 14:10–12; 2 Corinthians 5:8–11 NLT). This bit of information isn't given in scripture to instill fear or uncertainty in our hearts but rather so we can live our lives with confidence, knowing what's required to receive the full reward God has planned (2 John 1:8 NLT), a crown that lasts forever (1

Corinthians 9:25 NIV). Obviously, I'm not talking about a works-based salvation but the fruit of a life that's been redeemed. I don't know about you, but I often think about that day when I look upon the face of my Savior, and I want nothing more than to have something to present to Him that will bring Him the glory He deserves. At Golgotha, they placed a crown of thorns upon His head and mocked Him with chants of "Hail King of the Jews!" (John 19:3 NLT). One day, we'll have the honor of crowning Him with many crowns and joining with angelic hosts in declaring, "Holy! Holy! Holy!" (Revelation 4:8 NLT). *That*, friend, is the goal.

I don't know what the coming years will hold for Christians. However, according to research published in the most recent Open Doors World Watch List, the number of Christians detained or killed for their faith and the number of churches attacked or closed are all on the rise. In fact, statistics tell us that 360 million Christians, or one in seven believers around the world, suffers significant persecution for their faith. Every day, an average of more than sixteen believers are killed for following Jesus. With close to six thousand total martyrs, we've witnessed a 24 percent increase in Christians killed for the faith in just the past year. While I'm grateful that we continue to enjoy great religious freedoms in America, I think we'd be foolish to turn a blind eye to the growing levels of hostility being demonstrated toward Christians and the church online, in the media, and in certain sectors of society. There's a very real enemy at work here. As Paul tells us in Ephesians 2:2 (NKJV), the prince of the power of the air is at work in the lives of the disobedient. And as the disobedient increase in number, so too does his power and influence grow in our world.

According to a recent Pew Research Center survey, 47 percent of Christian adults in the United States say they believe "we are living in the end-times." Among evangelicals surveyed, 44 percent said they believe Jesus will return after a worsening of global conditions leads to a low point for humanity (a view consistent with a theological belief known as premillennialism), and 45 percent said that it's impossible to know the circumstances that will precede Jesus's return. Notice how few believe conditions will actually improve before the return of Christ. Now, to be clear, the point isn't that we need to predict what's going to happen. It's that we need to be prepared for whatever happens, and all indications are that we believers are in for a bumpy ride as our time in this world winds down. As Michael Tait has said, "In a world built on free will instead of God's will, we must be the freaks. While we may not be called to martyr our lives, we must martyr our way of life. We must put our selfish ways to death and march to a different beat. Then the world will see Jesus." In other words, we don't have the luxury to approach life any other way than to live as though Christ were returning tomorrow and souls hang in the balance today.

There are many Christians who are obsessed with the end-times and predicting the events that are prophesied to come. They invest enormous amounts of time and exhaust a ton of emotional energy in monitoring global events being reported by different news outlets. And they seem as though they're constantly fretting about a one-world government, the mark of the beast, and who the antichrist might be. Listen, if that's what our lives are marked by, then dare I say, we've missed the whole point and we've given Satan the upper hand already. As sons and daughters of God, we weren't meant to live in reaction to the schemes of darkness like puppets on a string. We must understand the devil uses fear as a motivator, but God uses love. We must be able to see this before we can ever see anything rightly. Like Jesus, you and I were made to live in response to the Father—to be led by His Spirit, compelled by love to fulfill both the great commandment (Matthew 22:37–40 NLT) and the great commission (Matthew 28:18–20 NLT). If you're looking for purpose, look no further! The Gospel makes it plain to understand, simple to obey.

As this book is brought to its end, I'd like to issue this call to action—instead of merely reading the Bible, let the Bible read you. Rather than asking God to bless whatever you're doing, go out and do what God has already said He'll bless. When faced with the choice to live for your own pleasure and glory or to die to yourself for His, choose the second option. Forget what you stand to lose and remind yourself of all there is to gain. Determine to daily walk in the footsteps of Jesus, along the Via Dolorosa (the painful road) toward Golgotha. Heed His solemn call and follow His clear example, becoming like a seed that falls to the ground and dies in order to produce many seeds (John 12:24 NIV). Death for the follower of Christ isn't our end but rather a beginning too beautiful for words, for it's the sacred place where the mind of Christ is found.

Printed in the United States
by Baker & Taylor Publisher Services